Thinking Out Loud
through
The American West

By
Leon "Pete" Sinclair

**MOUNTAIN
N'AIR BOOKS**
P.O. Box 12540
La Crescenta, CA
91224 - USA

Thinking Out Loud through the American West ©

By Leon "Pete" Sinclair

First Edition, 1999 Paper, printed on demand

Text copyright in 1999 by Leon "Pete" Sinclair

Published in the United States of America by
Mountain N' Air Books – P.O. Box 12540 – La Crescenta, CA 91224 USA

Phone: (800) 446-9696, (818) 951-4150 and (800)303-5578 fax

E-mail Address: mtnnair@aol.com

Cover and book layout/design by Gilberto d' Urso

Cover photo and Mr. Sinclair's picture by Kirk Sinclair

This book is an original paperback, published electronically and printed on demand.

Library of Congress Cataloging–in–Publication Data

Thinking Out Loud through the American West/ Leon Sinclair — 1st edtion

ISBN 1-879415-20-8

1. Sinclair, "Pete" Leon, 2. Western United States—mountaineering—travel adventure—environmental issues   essay

CIP

99-64214

ISBN 1-879415-20-8

TABLE OF CONTENTS

Preface

People who live in the American West know that we are privileged by the landscape. In 1958, out of the Army, out of money, and therefore out of school, I accepted the invitation of my classmate Barry Corbet to join him in Jackson's Hole, Wyoming for the winter. He wrote, "this town has the closest thing to a classless society that I have ever seen." That is less true now but forty years on I believe that what remains of American democratic ideals are purest in the West. Well-raised in New England I knew that with greater privilege comes greater responsibility. Seven months after moving to the West, a week after the summer solstice of 1959, in a cabin beside Don Sheldon's airstrip at the base of Denali, Mrs. Willett gave voice to this knowledge. Alaska was still a territory and largely unroaded. You got to Talkeetna by bush plane or by the railroad run by the US Department of Interior. It was the morning we came off the mountain. Mrs. Willett was feeding us breakfast, as she did all climbers who came off the mountain. We could not have refused had we wanted to, as we certainly did not. There were four of us, three of us there for the first time. With the addition of us three to the roster of all those who had climbed the mountain, the total did not yet come to three figures, fewer people than are now camped at Windy Corner on a single evening at the same time of year.

There was a lot of light in the cabin because of the solstice and also because of the unusual number of windowpanes for a cabin in the cold part of Alaska. It was a summer cabin. She was a schoolteacher in Anchorage during the winter. Even then they said of Anchorage that the best thing about it was it was only a half an hour from it to Alaska. I had a notion that Mrs. Willett—we knew not of a mister—was sweet on Sheldon. Sheldon, I learned a few days hence, was sweet on a long-legged, long dark-haired beauty who was herself a bush pilot out of Anchorage.

I don't remember how the topic arose, maybe it was the 55-gallon drums scattered over the tundra we'd seen from above on the flight out, but we got to talking about folks who came to Alaska to make their pile, tearing it up in the process if necessary.

"Yes," she said dismissively, "I say of such men, 'They violate the majesty of the country.'" I never forgot that phrase, obviously, but it isn't in my journal. I took it in with Mrs. Willett's waffles.

I found work and stayed in Alaska until the snow came in late September. That I had not committed that particular sin could not be a source of comfort. It meant only that I hadn't committed it *yet*.

My work as guide and photographer's assistant for Fritz Goro of *Life* took us all over the territory, I soon learned of another new sin, being a cheechako, a newcomer into the country. Years later I was outraged to discover that "cheechako" itself is not native to Alaska, but a derivation out of Nootka and Chinook, shipped up from Seattle by boat in some sourdough's word hoard with neither more nor less right to be there than I. Lusting for Alaska's mountains rather than her gold. It was too late to efface the notion that, in order not to violate the majesty of the country, I needed to know what the country required of me.

I was not innocent of the fact that we do not inhabit this country, particularly the West, as our ancestors, paired up from other countries, inhabited those countries. We can't assume that we belong where we are. I also knew that the West is still too big to be anything but explored. Among other things, this means that I as long as I didn't assume I belonged there, I could go anywhere, but I couldn't go everywhere. And finally I have learned that wherever the place in the West we choose to be, consideration is required of us because what we owe we learn from what we get. Knowledge of right doing in the West, though often a topic of debate, is ultimately the storied knowledge of experience.

Cannon Country

Introduction

Around age forty, most of us stumble onto the realization that
we are going to die. Later of course, much later, at fifty, I had
become accustomed to the notion that there would be an end to my
story, but that was all I was going to grant. There was no diminution
in my sense of exploration and adventure, although there was sense
enough not to confuse adventure with danger. In a fit of maturity I
told myself that my body was not the body of a twenty-five year old.
I then immediately set about denying it. Three weeks after my 50th
birthday I read a newspaper article about how, in the remaining five
weeks, a person could train to run in the upcoming Seattle Marathon.
Here I was, fifty years old and had never run a marathon, never realized that I had to! I got right on it. I had a fine time in the race,
finished in under four hours, as I had hoped. My fastest mile was the
last: proof that I had something left, was my interpretation.

After that little outburst, I began thinking about how to honor the
fact that I was half a century old. Still intact, I realized, were many of
the questions I had in 1960 about where was my place, what was its
nature if there were such a place, and what was I supposed to do. At
the time, me but a quarter of a century old, I believed that the answer
to these questions would come with the mere passing of time and
accumulation of experience. Now I had to admit that I needed a plan.

One thing I needed in the plan was a reason to go to California. In fifty years of living, over half of it in the West, I had never been to California. What was first just the circumstance that I needed to make a living and preferred living in the same town as the woman I loved, eventually became marked. Dear friends from college in New Hampshire and friends from Wyoming moved to California to live. Dear friends were *from* California. Somewhere along the line, what had been noticed became an *issue*. I myself entertained the thought that the reason I hadn't gotten to California yet was that I didn't want to have to climb El Capitan. Royal Robbins wrote me a letter from the LA Bus Station, suggesting that here was the perfect place for me to first see California. What began as me not having a reason to go to California became me having to have, increasingly, clear and compelling reasons *to* go there.

I can't imagine how I would have found a satisfactory reason to break my run-away record if my colleague, Sherburne (Jerry) Cook, a displaced Californian, hadn't told me about a lost cannon at the base of The Sierra Nevada. When a couple of my students began hunting for the cannon, I knew that I was never going to get a better reason or place to discover California.

Thanks Jerry.

Yellow Spot

On 12 June 1986, while standing on a boulder on the crest of a small outcropping at 38° 24' 26" north latitude and 119° 24' 30" west longitude, I became a cannon hunter. Looking northwest by north through a notch in the canyon wall of the West Walker River—eight miles away and 2000 feet below us—we could just see dried grass bright yellow against the gray-green of the sage, on the lower slopes of a ridge between the Antelope and Little Antelope Valleys. If we moved a few yards in any direction, the yellow patch was blocked. To our rear, on the eastern faces of the Sierra Nevada, shade moved swiftly and silently down the mountainside. The time, by interpolation from my field notebook and journal, was evening. Once again I failed to note the exact time. I am an imperfect predictor of what I later will wish to have noted of the present.

In a way, what brought us to the outcropping was an inexactitude in the journal of Lt. John Charles Fremont:

> January 29—From this height we could see, at a considerable distance below, yellow spots in the valley, which indicated that there was not much snow. One of these places we expected to reach to-night; and some time beingrequired to bring up the gun, I went ahead with Mr. Fitzpatrick and a few men, leaving the camp to follow, in charge of Mr. Preuss.

They did reach "one of these places," not that night but the next; the gun, a small brass cannon, didn't. This was the cannon we were hunting.

My companion cannon hunter, Trevor Peterson, was a former student of mine at The Evergreen State College. He had convinced me that it might be worthwhile to search for the cannon Fremont abandoned in the winter of 1844 during his search for a pass from the Great Basin to the Sacramento Valley. Thirty hours after leaving Olympia, we were having success. There were the "yellow spots," there remained only the matter of finding the cannon.

We would have been there sooner had Trevor not insisted that we stop at Reno, Virginia City, and Carson City for the reasons that I'd never been to these places and "they're part of cannon hunting." We stopped for a sumptuous cheap lunch at a casino in Reno. On the way past the last slot machine before the exit, it came to me that I'd never played a "slot" before. I was willing to bet that this was also part of cannon hunting. I put my quarter into the slot, pulled the lever and two quarters fell into the tray. "I've doubled my money and I'm quitting," I said to Trevor, I'll bet nobody else in Reno today will be able to say that." You'd think that in fifty years I'd have learned not to tempt the gods that way.

Trevor and I stood there in the yet warm evening, among a scattering of wildflowers germinated in the melt of the past winter's snow, looking from page to landscape and back again, reading both studiously. We were looking at Fremont's "Report of the Exploring Expedition to the Rocky Mountains in the Year 1842," and for "Oregon and Northern California in the Years 1843-'44," published in 1845 with the editorial help of his young, lovely, talented, and protective wife, Jessie Benton Fremont. If it were known how high the height, how considerable the distance, the cannon would have been defending the front lawn of a museum—as a cannon once thought to be Fremont's guards the museum in Carson City—and we would not have been there at that not-precisely-recorded moment in our search, our confidence growing that we knew one place where Fremont stood in his 31 mile crossing of the Sweetwater Mountains from the headwaters of the East Walker River to the headwaters of the West Walker River, a crossing that was being made because, essentially, the Pathfinder was, to say no more than what was precisely the case, turned around: going north after weeks of going south, looking for a place to go west. He wasn't lost exactly, his sextant told him that he was south of Sutter's place, but neither his sextant nor his mountain men and voyageur companions could find a pass for him. We were in country that Fremont would have gladly left for later expeditions, country not part of the Oregon Trail.

It is a good thing to know this about the early exploration of the American West—that the cannon was dispensable, but not the sextant and the journal. Our inhabitation of the American West has been a voyage to places found by Cook, Vancouver, Lewis and Clark, Wilkes and Fremont with their sextants, and the words written in their journals are both the ark and the flood of hopeful imagination washing over our worrying past.

On the drive down Trevor had said of various bits of Cascade landscape, "That's something like cannon country—only not quite."

"How not quite?"

"You'll see."

We were well-positioned to. Six miles distant from us at east northeast, and 3300 feet above, was the summit of the Sweetwater Mountains, the 11,673 foot Mt. Patterson. On around clockwise along the eastern horizon were the other ridges and summits of the Sweetwaters. Our view of Yosemite, to the south, was just blocked by the ridge that ran down to Devil's Gate. At southwest by west was Sonora Pass, a pass which failed to tempt Fremont. One mile directly west of us was Peak 8422, a height too modest to rate its own name but which has figured prominently in the speculations of cannon hunters.

We were in the ecotone between desert and alpine terrain, in the words of the *Report,* "It was pretty, open bottom, locked between lofty mountains. . . . We had now entirely left the desert country, and were on the verge of a region which, extended westward to the shores of the Pacific, abounds in large game, and is covered with a singular luxuriance of vegetable life." We were clearly in the verge, not in the singular luxuriance, but we were in the verge when it was as luxuriant, in a desert sort of way, as it can get. The dominant form of life, to the eye at least, was sagebrush—harboring a fair amount of grass and more than a dozen species of wildflowers then in bloom. There were small groves of aspen and pine along the streams and in the little gullies where ran seasonal rivulets of water.

It did not surprise me to have found this spot so quickly. Trevor had been cannon hunting for three years. He and fellow student, Michael Hardison, first searched for Fremont's cannon as a field project for a class. Their interests were not primarily in history: Trevor was at present in graduate school in architecture at the University of Washington in Seattle, and Michael was majoring in photography at Cal Arts. More attractive than the cannon, they subsequently confessed, were the nearby ski areas. However, once they started to work on the problem, they found they couldn't give it up. After graduation they continued their search and research whenever they could. After satisfying themselves that the cannon was probably still there to be found, they worked on establishing the route. The outcropping we were standing on was just yards from a line Trevor had drawn on a topographic map tracing his best guess as to Fremont's track.

When we arrived in cannon country we began our search by driving up through the West Walker River Canyon to Devil's Gate—not the Devil's Gate near Independence Rock in Wyoming and pictured in the *Report's* account of the first journey to the Rocky Mountains— this Devil's Gate could be thought of as either the pass between the valleys of the East and West Walker Rivers, or as the col between the Sweetwater Mountains and the Sierra Nevada, depending on whether it's the rivers or the mountains that have your attention. Since Fremont was still looking for the Buenaventura River at this point in his journey, "pass" is appropriately the term he uses:

January 27—Leaving the camp to follow slowly, with directions
    to Carson to encamp at the place agreed on, Mr. Fitzpatrick
    and myself continued the reconnaissance. Arriving at the
    head of the stream, we began to enter the pass—passing
    occasionally through open groves of large pine trees, on
    the warm side of the defile, where the snow had melted
    away, occasionally exposing a large Indian trail. Continu-
    ing along a narrow meadow, we reached in a few miles
    the gate of the pass, where there was a narrow strip of
    prairie, about fifty yards wide, between walls of granite

rock. On either side rose the mountains, forming on the left a rugged mass, or nucleus, wholly covered with deep snow, presenting a glittering and icy surface. At the time, we supposed this to be the point into which they were gathered between the two great rivers, and from which the waters flowed off to the bay. This was the icy and cold side of the pass, and the rays of the sun hardly touched the snow. On the left, the mountains rose into peaks; but they were lower and secondary, and the country had a somewhat more open and lighter character. On the right were several hot springs, which appeared remarkable in such a place. In going through, we felt impressed by the majesty of the mountain, along the huge wall of which we were riding. Here there was no snow; but immediately beyond was a deep bank, through which we dragged our horses with considerable effort. We then immediately struck upon a stream, which gathered itself rapidly, and descended quick; and the valley did not preserve the open character of the other side, appearing below to form a canyon. We therefore climbed one of the peaks on the right, leaving our horses below; but we were so much shut up, that we did not obtain an extensive view, and what we saw was not very satisfactory, and awakened considerable doubt. The valley of the stream pursued a northwesterly direction, appearing below to turn sharply to the right, beyond which further view was cut off. It was, nevertheless, resolved to continue our road the next day down this valley, which we trusted still would prove that of the middle stream between the two great rivers. Towards the summit of this peak, the fields of snow were four or five feet deep on the northern side; and we saw several large hares, which had on their winter color, being white as the snow around them.

The winter day is short in the mountains, the sun having but a small space of sky to travel over the visible part above our horizon; and the moment his rays are gone, the air is keenly cold. The interest of our work had detained us long, and it was after nightfall when we reached the camp.

Because Fremont was right in the middle of making his dyadic discovery that there is no Buenaventura River and there *is* a Great Basin, it is not clear what John Charles meant to signify by "the two great rivers," the San Joaquin and the Sacramento or the Colorado and Columbia. The considerable doubt that was awakened was the first stage in recognizing that none of the melt from the snow that encircled them (and would nearly kill and bury them in the month to come) ever reached the ocean. It is also not clear what he meant to signify by "the huge wall." The 200 foot outcroppings that flank the pass shouldn't be all that impressive to a person who'd seen the mountain country Fremont had seen.

This awakened in me a small doubt. There have been suggestions that Fremont or Jessie, while compiling this part of the *Report*, might have laid it on a little about the ruggedness of the terrain to help justify abandoning the cannon two days hence. On the other hand, many 19th Century descriptions of mountain landscapes are discomforting to 20th Century, post-Hemingway mountain travelers; we have toned-down colors on our rhetorical palettes. There were discrepancies between the *Report* and what was there on the ground, but this is not in itself alarming. If it was style, or even faulty memory, that generated the doubtful passages, the document is fundamentally reliable. There's all the difference in relying on a flawed journal as compared to a lying journal. Also, what looks tame from an automobile in June 1986 might look impressive from the back of a hungry, footsore horse in January 1844, with the Sierra Nevada in your face. Fremont is one of perhaps a dozen white men who had actually been on the summit of a real mountain of the American West, the peak in the Wind Rivers that bears his name. That gives him leave to call them as he sees them. But, he also knew that others will follow—composed the *Journal* and penned "the huge wall" precisely so that others would follow.

How are we to imagine the document being falsified? Would we have her say in her sweet Southern voice, "John Charles, Honey, would you say that you were ʻimpressed by the majesty of the mountain, along the huge wall of which you were riding'?"

And he in his deep manly voice, but teasing a little, "Ah sholy would?"

Perhaps his memory, working like a telephoto lens, foreshortened the scene so that the Sweetwaters become not part of the basin and range topography of Nevada, but buttress and rampart, the Sierras. The wall he saw in memory would then have been the abrupt eastern wall of the Sierra Nevada. This wall is still impressive.

We drove through the pass and continued south on 395 to where we could see east to the site of their encampment of the 25th and 26th in Bridgeport Valley, then turned around to begin retracing their route out of the valley. We could see the northeast corner of Yosemite National Park, clearly not a way for them to go. Our first stop was Swauger Creek, the probable site of their camp of the 27th.

Looked like a place to camp all right.

Gliding north on newly paved 395 through the pass, past Fales Hot Springs, we came to a gravel road that took us across a gently rising plateau called Burcham Flat to a crest that examination of a topographic map revealed to be the north ridge of the second largest peak in the Sweetwater Mountains, Wheeler Peak. A dirt track took us east along this ridge for a quarter of a mile. A grass track took us sixty yards down the north slope of the ridge, where we parked the car. A game trail took us up the outcropping where we spotted the yellow spots and were suddenly taken back in time, but only 143 years, three or four grandfathers ago. Our past is very close to us.

We descended the outcropping to return to our time, but not entirely.

"That barking sound . . ."

"Yeah, I've been hearing it off and on for a while now."

"At first I thought it was a sheep dog."

"It's a mountain lion."

"I wondered."

"Technically I believe it's called a cough, the cough of the cougar."

"Lewis doesn't mention a mountain lion. He mentions a bear . . . and ants, fierce ants."

A Guidebook

Ernest Allen Lewis is the author of "The Fremont Cannon: High Up and Far Back," the book that sent Trevor and Michael cannon hunting. The road we were on traversed the east side of Peak 8422. Lewis thinks the cannon is somewhere on the west, the river side, of 8422. Another cannon-hunter, the late Fred I. Green, whose correspondence forms the bulk of the file at the museum in Carson City, argues that 8422 was the height that Fremont and Fitzpatrick climbed to scout the country. Trevor had tested both views on the ground, wasn't satisfied by the fit of either and designed a view of his own.

The hollow is an oblong bowl one mile across at its widest point by two and a half miles long—averaging 400 feet in depth. We stopped at the low point of the lip of the hollow, a sort of English saddle between the canyon of the West Walker River, 1200 feet below us to the west, and Cottonwood Meadow, 300 feet below us in the hollow. To our left was the gorge Cottonwood Creek has cut through the ridge drops down from the double summits of the Sweetwater Mountains, Mount Patterson and Wheeler Peak. As we could tell from our topographic map, on the other end of the gorge Cottonwood Creek joined Deep Creek a mile upstream of where Deep Creek enters the West Walker River. It is this precious, sweet water, water that made for the singular luxuriance that Fremont noted, that Los Angelinos are sucking out of the Great Basin with their pipeline syphon.

Cottonwood Creek then, leaves its gentle meadow in the hollow, cuts through the ridge that forms the north lip of the hollow, bends sharply west to merge with Deep Creek in its canyon and drops a thousand feet in two miles to reach the bottom of the West Walker River Canyon. Trevor's hypothesis was that—confronted with the choice of plunging into the gorge at the north end of the hollow or hauling it westward up to the rim where we were standing—Fremont's men abandoned the cannon.

January 29 [continued] We followed a trail down a hollow where
the Indians had descended, the snow being so deep that
we never came near the ground; but this only made our
descent the easier, and, when we reached a little affluent
to the river at the bottom, we suddenly found ourselves in
presence of eight or ten Indians. They seemed to be watching our motions, and, like the others, at first were indis-
posed to let us approach, ranging themselves like birds on
a fallen log on the hill side above our heads, where, being
out of reach, they thought themselves safe. Our friendly
demeanor reconciled them, and, when we got near enough,
they immediately stretched out to us handfuls of pine nuts,
which seemed an exercise of hospitality. We made them a
few presents, and, telling us that their village was a few
miles below, they went on to let their people know what
we were. The principal stream still running through an
impracticable canyon, we ascended a very steep hill, which
proved afterwards the last and fatal obstacle to our little
howitzer, which was finally abandoned at this place.

The cannon might be 50 yards from where we were standing. The
fallen log too. Ah yes, "they thought themselves safe." Well why not,
they were about to be bequeathed a howitzer.

The brush was thick inside the entrance of the little gorge to Deep
Creek, making an excellent place for a cannon to hide. Trevor thought
the cannon might be there; it was one of the few places he hadn't
looked. That seemed reasonable to me. It also seemed reasonable that
they might have abandoned the cannon earlier. It depends on what
you make of "this place." And "hollow." And "little affluent." And
so forth. Did they try to hide the cannon with Indians watching?
Hmmn. As Wittgenstein observes, explanations have to stop somewhere. We'd know more when we found the cannon.

Lewis believed that "the river" and "the principle stream" were
the same water course, the West Walker River. Trevor found Fremont's
uses of "stream" and "river" to be consistently distinct. I thought

Trevor had got it right. It had been a fortuitous confirmation of Trevor's hypothesis that the outcropping where we saw the yellow spots is only yards from where Trevor had sited the camp, and the spots are visible from there too. There were before us two candidates for the "affluent." Coming into the southeast corner of the hollow were two canyons containing the South and North Forks of Cottonwood Creek. That these forks both came into the hollow from the south suggests that these tributaries were not named from the God's eye perspective of the cartographer but the ridge and canyon perspective of the miner or prospector.

We could see a dozen groves of trees and two or three dozen thickets of brush in the hollow worthy of search—assuming that Fremont's men hid not buried the cannon. The best reason for assuming they didn't bury the canon was that we came here to search the groves and thickets and had brought no shovels and picks or digging bars. The second best reason that they probably did not bury the cannon is the fact that they were here in January not June.

A mile along the rim the road swung down into the canyon of Deep Creek, about the meanest little canyon in the area. We stopped to take a look. The Pathfinder had to be better at it than that. He likely didn't go down into the canyon of Deep Creek, just worked his way down off the rim, reaching the West Walker at a place now called Shingle Mill Flat. The road winds seven miles down the lower western slopes of the Sweetwater Range, skirting the river canyon, into Antelope Valley and the town of Walker. We stopped in at the general store.

On Trevor and Michael's first trip, Fremont's mention in the journal of: "the steep ascents and deep snow exhausting both men and animals;" and Lewis's: "Persons with bad hearts, high blood pressure or poor muscle tone should not actively take part in a search because of the high altitude and treacherous terrain;" had them expecting to be searching in some remote part of the Sierra Nevada known only to a few of the hardier frontier history buffs, the ones with buckskin suits and muzzle-loading rifles. When they stopped in Walker to get some help in orienting themselves to the country, they were not surprised that the lady in the general store would not know where Peak 8422 was.

They *were* surprised when, at the mention of Fremont, she said, "Oh, you want to drive on up 395 here until you hit the Fremont-Carson Route." The Fremont-Carson Route was the gravel forest service road we'd been following.

Packed in coolers in the trunk of the car were a couple of cases of very good ale, porter and bitters from a Seattle micro brewery. Trevor, as best man, was transporting this to Michael's wedding. This precious cargo had to be kept cool because it was made without preservatives. After replenishing the ice we went up canyon on 395 along the West Walker River, stopping at Shingle Mill Flat to look at the place where Fremont descended to the river. There was no need for us to retrace that part of his route since, by everybody's account, the cannon had been abandoned long before. We continued on up 395 to our camp.

We camped on a narrow grassy area between the highway and the Little West Walker River, an acknowledged camping spot rather than an official campsite. There were no constructed fire pits, picnic tables, or toilets. Only a newspaper dispenser for the Sacramento Bee showed that we were expected. While we'd been up finding the hollow, a camping trailer and a car camper had squeezed in on either side of us, negating the effort we had made to avoid crowding the three camper/trailer rigs and travel trailer that formed an aluminum fortification along the bank. Although we were in there cheek to jowl, the roar of the river provided a batting of sound that afforded us auditory privacy at least. The spring run-off must have been subsiding, but fording the river would have been difficult and dangerous, even here on one of the few flat spots in the canyon.

This thought didn't occur to me until we had been out of the car for a bit. In the car, I'd forgotten that a river is as formidable a barrier as a mountain range, and more dangerous. Many more emigrants died crossing rivers than were killed in crossing the mountains or deserts, or by Indians. While we waited for it to get dark enough to sleep, I perused Lewis's book. I came upon an account I had overlooked. I became raptly attentive:

> Harry Tom, a Maidu Paiute Indian, was a guide for hunters who came to Mono County seeking wild game. Tom

was widely respected for his athletic ability, sagacity and honesty. In October of 1936, he was closely examining the old 1881 Irvin cannon in front of the Mono County Courthouse at Bridgeport, when Ella M. Cain stopped to talk with him. Ella asked why he was so interested in an old relic that he had walked by hundreds of times. Matter-of-factly he replied, "Oh, it looks a lot like the one I saw out in the mountains a few years ago." Mrs. Cain's interest was immediately piqued. At the time she was Mono County's foremost historian, a former school teacher, and perhaps the area's most respected lady. She was acutely aware of the history of the Fremont cannon and the many sagas and legends surrounding its mystique. She pressed Tom for more information: Where did he see the cannon? When? Was anyone with him? "It was the 1928 hunting season, I think," he said. "I was guiding some flatlanders, riding the low side of the hill trying to scare deer up to the hunters riding the ridge above me. About noon, I stopped to rest my horse and there it was—back in a brushy area in a thick little grove of trees. I kind of shoved my way in to take a good look at it." Tom further described the cannon's carriage as being in bad shape. One wheel was broken and the other almost buried. And, the wood was brittle and crumbly with age. "But, it sure looked a lot like this one," he said again.

"Did you ever tell anyone about it," Ella asked?

"Not that I remembered, never had any reason to," Tom replied. Harry Tom's nickname was "Silent Tom," because he seldom had anything to say and, as was the nature of the time, he had few friends outside the Indian population.

Ella's continued questioning of Harry Tom revealed that he wasn't too sure of the exact location because he and the hunters had covered a lot of ground in the days following. And, frankly, he hadn't given much thought to the cannon. He reminded Ella that with all of his other duties, such as setting up camp, caring for the horses, cooking meals, skinning the deer and bears killed, bagging and caring for the meat, breaking camp, and all the other jobs that go with his work, the cannon faded from his mind. It didn't seem that important. Tom did ask one favor of Ella, "please don't tell this to anyone but your husband. I don't want to be known as another 'drunk' who saw a cannon."

Trevor was somewhat less taken with this account than I, "If you want reports of cannon sightings," he said, "look in that box of stuff I copied from the file—and that's only part of it."

After a micro-pause to wonder if the roles of professor and student weren't being reversed, I barged ahead. True, this was only one of many reports of cannon sightings, as Lewis also points out, but this one, "is worth repeating here because of the uncommon veracity of the people involved, and because there is logic in its substance." I wasn't sure what Lewis was referring to as the logic in its substance, but I knew what he meant by uncommon veracity. "Uncommon veracity" is precisely the phrase Boswell used in his journal to describe what he perceived, on first meeting him, to be the central character trait of Captain James Cook. It gave me great confidence that Lewis had placed Ella and Harry Tom in Cook's company.

What an economy of effort was being offered here! This story of sighting a cannon leapt over decades of messy and contradictory history about what happened to Fremont's cannon. Fremont abandoned a cannon in 1844, Harry Tom spotted one in 1928. What's to know about what happened in between? Should Harry Tom's cannon turn out to be the wrong type, that would be time enough to take on the rumors, fanciful newspaper accounts, frauds, and political complexities. How much nobler a discovery it would make to track John Charles Fremont, Kit Carson, and Thomas "Broken-Hand" Fitzpatrick into the mountains, into a hollow, into a cottonwood grove, and there find the cannon almost completely covered except for the carrying handle that distinguishes the Fremont cannon from all others.

The other thing Harry Tom's story did was narrow the scope of the search to what could be seen on the low side of a hill by a man on horseback.

"How will we get the cannon out?"

"I wonder if that prospector with the mules camped on Deep Creek is a cannon hunter too? Maybe we could work something out with him."

Searching for Terrain and Character

At 0730 the next morning we were in Bridgeport, having first left camp at 0530 that morning and driven up to the hollow to pick a place to search. My interpretation of the landscape was that we should start searching at the south rim and search the entire hollow. As I understood the situation there were three categories of evidence, three "texts," to be interpreted:

> First and second-hand accounts made by the expedition members and people they talked to at the time.
> Everybody else's account at any time.
> The landscape itself.

I had at least amateur qualifications to read the primary and secondary texts, but I came to cannon country to interpret the third, for the chance to read the landscape and thereby use a skill I hadn't used for years. In Fremont's party were Kit Carson and Tom "Broken-Hand" Fitzpatrick, two of the all time great interpreters of the landscape of the American West. Fremont himself was not a mountain man but one of our first mountaineers. I had done some mountaineering myself in what seemed like a former age. Still, reading the landscape is one of the mountaineering skills that doesn't have to diminish with age. I believed that I might be able to stand where Fremont, Carson and Fitzpatrick stood and know what they were thinking about what they saw. I believed that the landscape might prove to be the most reliable of the three texts: possessing, as it does, character but not motive.

I had worked as a professional climber (meaning that I did it for money, implying nothing about ability) well into my thirties. Working with people much younger, stronger, and more skilled than I taught me to be wily. Although my search plan had us starting where the cannon probably wasn't and moved toward where Trevor thought the cannon might be, this plan had two great advantages: it gave the appearance of thoroughness and it was all downhill.

Trevor didn't object, but since we didn't know how long it might take to search all the wrong places that led downhill toward the right place, and we needed gas, he suggested that we get gas first.

As we drove toward the highway along the Fremont Carson Route, I tried to pick a route for sixty horses and mules and thirty men to cross the lower slopes of the Sweetwaters, not in the soft light of the spring dawn, but in the crystal hard clarity of winter at that altitude: "Snow and broken country together made our traveling difficult: we were often compelled to make large circuits, and ascend the highest and most exposed ridges, in order to avoid snow, which in other places was banked up to a great depth." It was difficult to form the picture not because it was the wrong season, but because the whump-whump-whump of the tires negotiating the ruts kept knocking my attention off the mark. It just wasn't useful to attend to the details of the route while in the car.

On the other hand, the car on smooth road was a good place to watch the landscape drift by the windows and have reveries. My reverie, as we glided down into Bridgeport on 395, was about my first attentive look at the country the day before. The lengthened shadows and ameliorated light of evening in cannon country put me in mind of the mountainous terrain of Southeast Wyoming. Since I moved to Puget Sound I've had periodic bouts of homesickness for the high, dry mountains. We lived in a cabin at the base of the Medicine Bow Range where from the porch we could see the Laramie Mountains 30 miles to the east and the Colorado Rockies the same distance to the south. A few years ago I saw a photograph of that country in a whisky ad that caused me to dig out my old cowboy boots and wear them the next day, with umbrella accessory—making a picture of me. I didn't care; I was in grief at having lost sun and sky. The same nostalgia for the landscape at head of the Little Laramie River seizes my wife—

curiously, because for her, a native of Jackson Hole, there are no mountains but the Tetons. We say it is the sky that we miss, knowing it is more but not what.

However infusions of memory colored my understanding of cannon country, there was perfect clarity about its structure and texture—and this was the one disharmony in our prospect. The country was so open that, if the cannon were out there, we should have been able to see the grove or thicket concealing it. It was, in other words, a wonderful place to look for a cannon, but an unlikely place for a cannon to hide for 142 years.

Since we were in town anyway, why not have breakfast.

We drove clear through town to the junction of Highway 395 and the road north to Willmington, Nevada. There's a Devil's Gate on that road too, where the East Walker River crosses the Nevada border—you can't get to Bridgeport from the north without going through a Devil's Gate. The Hays Street Cafe had just opened, or reopened. Entrance was from the parking lot not the street, which, once past the cafe, was highway out of town. The building was mounted, perhaps recently, on a two and a half foot foundation, necessitating a handicapped access ramp that had to use most of the front of the building to have a sufficiently gentle slope.

The inside was paneled with real wood and trimmed with a wide board painted forest green. The upper half of the wall was sort of eggshell white with a wide green strip of wallpaper trim around the top of the wall. The formica tops of the ten tables were the same solid green as were the heavy cotton curtains. The building was close to square and the floor plan was simple: the front half was the dining area; the restrooms were back left; and we looked at the gleaming stainless steel and white kitchen through the waitresses' serving area, which served as a buffer between the dining room and the kitchen. According to Trevor, who worked in a restaurant to support his education habit, the equipment was the very best. The serving area's counter was overarched with an eighteen foot plant shelf completely full of plants with congratulatory notes attached. The chairs were captain's chairs, substantial but not stolid. In the southwest corner was a large oil painting of a mountain ranch cabin in the winter. If the fence in the scene had been buck and rail instead of post and pole, the scene could have been of the Rockies.

The place had a quality that was distinctly personal and—though the cook was a large bearded man—feminine, though it was hard to see why feminine. There was no lace, no pink or baby-blue or cheery yellow; there was a good eye for proportion, line, light and color. Whatever it was that made it seem feminine was in the combination. It seemed a place made by a woman who unapologetically domesticates with what she has at hand as she has to, a woman, who as needed, would give her horse a caress or break her crop over his goddamned neck should he refuse a fence.

We sat in the southwest corner in ample light admitted by the large windows. They were not picture windows but small-paned windows, no illusion of being outside, an assertion of insidedness in her dining room and kitchen. When we looked out the windows we saw the town and country over the rooftops of the cars, from horseback height. Trevor ordered a cinnamon roll because he made cinnamon rolls at four a.m. at the restaurant where he worked. The Hays Street Cafe cinnamon rolls were tiny. That confirmed a suspicion that Trevor had that these people didn't know about running a restaurant. They obviously weren't trying to skimp, they just didn't know that cinnamon rolls are supposed to cover a dessert plate. Trevor never thinks about calories. He said, "This place won't be here the next trip we make down here."

Noting without comment that Trevor was admitting the possibility that this might not be the final search, I said:

"Why?"

"Look at the money they've spent on remodeling. And the equipment. Even worse, they've got too many people working here."

I hoped he was wrong; and so, I suspect did Trevor. The Hays Street Cafe was the only newly designed restaurant I'd been in lately that felt as if the designer was more concerned with pleasing me than manipulating me. The restaurant made a quiet place in the mind from which to look out upon the country.

We started our search at 0900 and were back at the car well-sweated at 1402. I asked Trevor if it would be all right if we moved our camp to some place further from the exhaust fumes, roar, and lights of the highway and from the crowd, roar, and damp of our site along the river. Again he humored the old fellow.

Up 395 to the head of the canyon, where the highway turned from west to south, we continued west on a gravel road, Cow Camp Road, and went on up the Little Walker for three miles to a forest service camp in a grove of aspen and pinon pine. Obsidian Campground, as it was called, hadn't officially opened yet. There was no piped water, just river water, but there were campsites with tables, fireplaces, and numbers, and there were pit toilets. These modest amenities pleased me in a manner that I would have scorned in my mountain man days. I reckoned I was still at least a medium-hard man but I had ceased to be entertained by surviving on rawhide, flint and steel, a Swiss Army knife, a Sierra Club cup, and a hunk of pemmican. (And maybe an Eddie Bauer down jacket and sleeping bag.)

We wrote in our field journals while waiting for the ale to warm, and, when it had, convened a meeting to hard-headedly discuss our prospects. We could afford to have a hard-headed conference because it was clear that no analysis or conclusion could prevent us from having fun. Our site was right at the edge of the five-acre grove containing the campground. Through the branches of the aspens we had a picture postcard view of the summit of Mount Emma—upon whose flanks we were camped. The atmosphere was of the type prescribed by physicians for nervous disorder. The wind was light. The sky was cloudless. The temperature was temperate. The mixture of piney woods and sage—cushioned by the scents rising from sun-warmed lichen, grasses, and wildflowers—put one in mind of all the first days of summer vacations. That morning we had searched swales, meadows and hillsides and groves perfectly contrived for cannon hunting: thick enough to conceal a cannon from the uneager eye but not so thick as to incommode our pleasant meanderings through the hollow.

I wanted to talk about Harry Tom. We, or at least I, welcomed the focusing properties of the story at the beginning of our search that morning. But, as our search continued, I felt constrained by the hill-bottom, horse-back height prescription.

Tomorrow we would work on Trevor's site for the cannon. It would not be fair to arbitrarily limit where we looked while testing his hy-pothesis. We needed to review our reasons for believing that Harry Tom had seen Fremont's cannon. We had excellent reasons for wish-ing the story true:

If Harry Tom had seen the cannon in 1928, that meant it hadn't been melted down in 1918 to make new cannon for the war of that moment. And it meant that the cannon hadn't been buried, or found.

When hardheaded, one notes that Lewis tries overhard to establish Harry Tom's veracity. There's a photograph of Harry Tom in Lewis's book with the caption:

> HARRY TOM, 'CHIEF WHITE WING When this Maidu-Paiute Indian claimed to have seen the "Fremont Cannon" and described it, no one ever doubted or questioned the veracity of his claim.
>
> Born in Yosemite about 1895, he made a good living as a guide for hunters, fishermen and mountain enthusiasts. He was probably the best athlete ever to live in Mono County. A husky and wiry 5-foot-5-inches, he was a cham-pion bronc rider and rodeo performer with an uncanny ability to train horses and mules; the fastest runner and longest jumper in all contests; and an exceptional boxer. Indians and Whites came for miles to watch his war dances.
>
> He died in 1979 in his beloved Antelope Valley, and is buried in the Indian Cemetery at Coleville.

It takes a skeptical soul to disbelieve a man with those credentials when the man is staring you right in the eye from the page of a book. I don't know that I could be any more convinced if I knew that he played bridge and his handicap in golf. But, why didn't Ella Cain find the cannon? The story goes that she got sick and then busy with a more sedentary life—and she wasn't all that fond of the out-of-doors to begin with. Fair enough. But if, as Lewis believes was the case, Ella had meant to keep her promise to Harry Tom that she wouldn't tell anybody what he told her because he didn't want to be known as a drunk with a cannon story, and that's why she never told anybody where Harry Tom said the cannon was, why do we now have the story at all? If Ella had just sent a friend out to pick up the cannon, Harry Tom would be remembered as the wonderful guy who first spotted the cannon, and liked to have a drink now and then too.

I once overheard a remark that comes back to me at times like this: "My old man used to say that if you listen long enough you'll hear it the way you want it."

Now that we were away from the trucks on the highway and were further from the river, we couldn't ignore the jets. The jet sounds were very odd. When a jet came over we had been glancing up and resuming what we were doing, as if we lived near an airport. Now there came the sound of three jets. We looked up and around and back at each other, and up and around again, and realized that we, heads full of sound, could not only not find these jets, but had not yet seen even one jet— though the jets had not been clearing the summits of the Sierras by much, and, in this present instance, not at all, but were weaving around over the headwaters of the East and West Carson Rivers. We said:

"What *are* those things? That's not any jet *I* ever heard before."

"They must be the latest thing, invisible."

"How far are we from Edwards Air Force Base?"

"Not too far for these guys, but there's another place over in Nevada, just about straight east of us."

"This seems to be the place for the latest in weapons. Fremont says the French just invented his cannon for their war in Algeria."

Terrain, Character and Text

There were sixteen people eating and six people working at the Hays Street Cafe Saturday morning. Perhaps they were expecting a busy day; mine already seemed so.

The rough three-mile drive on Cow Camp Road from our camp out to the highway did not shake me loose from the dream I'd had in the night. My point of view in the dream was 3/4 of the way up the hill of the main street in Virginia City looking down from, oddly, sitting, not standing, height. It was precisely the spot from which

Virginia City would seem most garish, and, to make the point more telling, my dream poet had thrown in some store fronts of souvenir shops that I recognized as being from Jackson, Wyoming and West Yellowstone, Montana before those towns had gotten so high toned. There were scores of people on the boardwalks, as many as could move in a serene, stately, but purposeful tread from store to store, in and around and out, pausing and musing over this and that and moving on. There was a glimpse of a woman who purchased something, a wrapped package was on the counter, and she was standing immobile, waiting for her change. Her countenance expressed that her purchase was nice enough, worth having, but just not quite it. Back out on the street, in spite of the fact that Virginia City was crowded, the vision was not of frenetic activity but of implacability so stubborn that it made me laugh out of my dream. I work with a dream psychologist from time to time. A sometimes consequence of this is that an interpretation of a dream attaches itself to a dream so quickly that it kind of runs together with the dream. I woke up identifying day residue: our stop in Virginia City and the thought, "What *energy* we have; we never stop looking." The thought made me sentimental. A tear ran across the bridge of my nose and another one leaked out of the outside corner of my other eye and plopped loudly on the nylon of my sleeping bag. As I said, medium-hard.

On the smooth highway into Bridgeport, words came to me from twenty years before, the words of a fellow graduate student, Tony Voss. Tony described to me, in his British South African voice, how moved he had been during a visit to the Mormon genealogical library by "the sight of all those people, us, we colonials, searching the shelves for signs of ourselves." And I in Virginia City had been moved by the thought that, if Mark Twain is the father of American literature, then Virginia City, this mining town born of greed, lust, and desperation was the birthplace of American literature, not, as he and Libby might have wished to think, Hartford.

In spite of the two teardrops, it was a cheering dream presaging a happy day of searching through the clumps of Artemisia and groves of cottonwood and pine, beginning in what had become my favorite cafe, which I already had found.

At 1035 we were trudging up the Fremont Carson Route on our way to the rim of the hollow and our car—having traversed the Deep Creek Cut from Cottonwood Meadow, and having abandoned in the cut the hypothesis Trevor had held for a year.

Ten minutes after entering the canyon we had covered all the terrain to which mules might have gotten a cannon. In about two and a half more minutes, we had covered all the additional terrain to which the whole party might have dragged a cannon they were looking to abandon. Then from there until we exited from the cut, it was scree right down to narrow stream banks, cliff-base scree alternating with gully-base scree. It was theoretic—ally possible for Preuss to have gotten the cannon to the first of these scree slopes, and since these were the only unstable terrain on or near the route, we could permit ourselves to imagine that the cannon was buried underneath it. If we haven't found the cannon in ten years or so, maybe we'll take a look.

When I told my academic colleagues what I was about, nearly all of them had the same first question: "Do you have a metal detector?" A colleague who'd done some mining exploration in Canada told me about a detector that could be suspended from a small plane. I responded that we could always rent one. But I was not long in cannon country before becoming convinced that using technological magic was not the way to play this game. Even though I wasn't totally certain as to what this game was really about, it was clear that the cannon not an end but a confirmation. No *deus ex machina* would be needed to bring this drama to a conclusion. This was about figuring it out not about getting lucky.

After we'd gone about 200 yards into the cut we stopped looking for the cannon. Instead we followed a game trail. I so enjoyed keeping to the trail—picking it up where it got faint by remembering how a deer would go, looking ahead to guess the problems the trail would be anticipating, giving up or gaining height to get an advantage on a obstacle to come—that I would not let Trevor in the lead. I took unseemly pride in losing the trail only once and in not having to break stride more than half a dozen times in a mile, the pride of learning to make yourself at home in a place obviously not designed for humans.

I sometimes wonder if it is a good sign that we go so far afield in an effort to be at home where we weren't meant to be. The only way I can think of to find out is to do it until I know.

By the time we got back to the car, I had formulated a new theory: the cannon was in the canyon of the South Fork of Cottonwood Creek. Forming a new theory about where the cannon might be is not difficult to do. There are essentially five allusions in the *Report* that approximate fact nearly enough to be taken as reliable clues. In order of declining precision they are: 1) a wind-cleared height where they might have camped on the 28th, from which they could see the yellow spots, 2) the hollow that they followed the Indians down, 3) the affluent-stream-river-impracticable canyon configuration, 4) the steep hill which proved to be the last and fatal obstacle and 5) the hillside where eight or ten Indians ranged themselves above their heads like birds on a log. The steep hill and plausibly Indian-besat hillsides fit so many spots in the terrain as to make these last two features seem virtually portable. To make a new story of where the route went, you find a place with one of the top three (height, branched-stream, hollow) in combination with the other two. Move their route to that place and Lo! there will be a steep hill and a place for eight or ten Indians to sit. It's like playing five card stud when everybody has two wild cards in their hand.

I moved their camp while standing on our old viewpoint in the saddle on the north rim. We had parked just below it. It was easy. I looked south across the hollow and lifted the camp from its old height to the right (west) of the outcropping and carried it eastward a half mile across a knoll to a height only five hundred feet higher than it was on in its old position. The hollow remained the same and the stream.

My authority for this move:

January 28—To-day we went through the pass with all the camp, and, after a hard day's journey of twelve miles, encamped on a high point where the snow had been blown off, and the exposed grass afforded a scanty pasture for the animals. Snow and broken country together made our traveling difficult: we were often compelled to make large cir-

cuits, and ascend the highest and most exposed ridges, in
order to avoid snow, which in other places was banked up
to a great depth.

It described the new site as well as the old, but, unfortunately,
several other places too. Half a mile out of the way and five hundred
feet of unnecessary height is what I considered to be, after three hours
and twenty minutes of hiking, a reasonable quantity of circuity.

Perhaps to reassure ourselves that there were features of the route
that were solid, we returned to 395 and drove down the West Walker
River to where we thought they had joined it from above. That eight
mile drive brought us again to Sawmill Flat, abreast of and 800 feet
downhill from where we started. There was a logging road which
gained three hundred and fifty-three feet of altitude up the opposite
canyon wall. From the end of the road we had a good view of the
lower third of the route down from the rim of the hollow. It was
reassuringly obvious.

We went the Walker Store for ice was next. The lady half recognized Trevor, "Fishing or just hiking around?"

"Cannon hunting," said Trevor.

"Oh. There was a fellow in here a while ago who was doing that.
He had a book—I've forgotten who wrote it..."

"Lewis?"

"Yes, that could be it, probably was. Anyway this fellow said that
the gentleman who wrote the book had some real good information
from an Indian. I asked him, 'What Indian?' and he says..."

"'Harry Tom,'" I interjected, taking the part of the cannon hunter
fellow.

She nodded and went on, "Well I *knew* Harry Tom and I told him,
'Good luck if the fellow that wrote your book got his information
from Harry Tom.'"

"Uh oh," said Trevor.

She went on, "There's nothing an Indian likes better than to fool a
white man." She said this, I thought, in the manner of a local being
kind to greenhorns, who, she suspected, might have another view for
which we could be forgiven because we are without experience in this

matter.

It was a good thing that we were back at the camp early because we had a lot of "theorizing," as we called it, to do, theorizing of the loosest kind. The lady at the general store had made explicit the question of Harry Tom's motive for telling the story he told. There were others to consider; Ella Cain's motive for believing it, Lewis's, ours. There's a certain amount of entertainment in guessing about a person's motives—you feel real smart when you've nailed someone's hidden agenda—but it can get to be a logical swamp in which you eventually feel turned around and in it knee deep. Questions of motive are questions of character. And, when remarking upon a character whose owner can no longer challenge you to a duel, the rules go slack. This is how Lewis pictures the abandoning of the cannon:

> The next morning, while the cannon party was going back down the south face of Mt. 8422 to retrieve the howitzer, Fremont, Fitzpatrick, and a few others rode down the north face of the mountain along a gradual trail to the river. As he talked with a group of Washoe Indians, Fremont looked around at the rugged ice and snow covered canyon. Knowing the cannon could go no farther, he sent a messenger, perhaps Kit Carson, back to the camp with this welcome news. The courier probably arrived in camp at about the same time as the cannon party returned with the cannon. It was a jubilant group that rode away from the little howitzer, sitting atop its carriage in a small meadow on this high, wind-swept mountain on the edge of the Sierra Nevada. They probably did try to cache the 500 pounds of ammunition, but they probably made no attempt to conceal or dismantle the cannon. They just rode away.

This is a plausible characterization given Fremont's account, except that: *"It was a jubilant group that rode away from the little howitzer...."* couldn't have come from Fremont. Fremont says:

> The other division of the party did not come in to-night, but encamped in the upper meadow, and arrived the next morning. They had not succeeded in getting the howitzer

beyond the place mentioned, and where it had been left by
Mr. Preuss in obedience to my orders; and, in anticipation
of the snow banks and snow fields still ahead, foreseeing
the inevitable detention to which it would subject us, I
reluctantly determined to leave it there for the time. It was
of the kind invented by the French for the mountain part
of their war in Algiers; and the distance it had come with
us proved how well it was adapted to its purpose. We left
it, to the great sorrow of the whole party, who were grieved
to part with a companion which had made the whole distance from St. Louis, and commanded respect for us on
some critical occasions, and which might be needed for
the same purpose again.

Lewis's description of the mood of the men when abandoning the
canon is so contrary to Fremont's that I believe that Lewis would not
have dared tell the story the way he has if Fremont were alive. And
Lewis is a Fremont partisan.

Lewis is not acting completely independent of all authority. Some
chroniclers of Fremont's life and times have not hesitated to question
his character. Most of the questions stem from events later in his life—
usually political events in which Fremont's choice of action was one
disapproved of by one of two of California's early intellectuals, the
philosopher Royce and the historian Bancroft, who's dislike of John
Charles seems chemical rather than scholarly in origin.

If we ignore his illegitimate birth, and set aside the story of the
twenty-eight year old John Charles eloping with the seventeen year
old Jessie, there is nothing to fault John Charles about until the beginning of this, the second expedition to the Rockies.

On or about 8 May 1843, Fremont put in a requisition for the
mountain howitzer. The commanding officer of the St. Louis Arse-
nal, Capt. William H. Bell, issued the howitzer only after being ordered to do so by the commander of the Third Military Department, Stephen Watts Kearny. On the tenth, Capt. Bell wrote to his
boss in the Ordinance Office in Washington, Col. George Talcott,
to say that he had obeyed the "positive order" reluctantly and "if in

this matter I have erred, I hope the colonel will perceive that it has been in consequence of being placed in a dilemma of some difficulty and that it has been from a want of anything but a respect for the order and regulations of my department." Captain Bell, his ass well-covered, could then sit back and watch the fun. *His* character, at least, is perfectly transparent.

The matter went leap-frogging up the chain of command so quickly—Fremont over Bell to Kearny, Bell over Kearny to Washington—as to suggest that the issue was personal and political rather than the good order of the department. It soon went through the War Department to the desk of James M. Porter, the Secretary of War (as we called them then), soon enough for him to make an inquiry of Fremont's boss, J.J. Abert, Colonel of the Corps of Topographical Engineers. Colonel Abert's responded that small arms but not a howitzer were the appropriate arms for the sort of expedition Fremont was on. Colonel Abert then immediately wrote to his subordinate:

Sir.

From the reports which have reached the Bureau in reference to the arrangements which you are making for the expedition to the Rocky Mountains, I fear that the discretion and thought which marked your first expedition will be found much wanting in the second.

The limit placed upon your expenditures by the orders of this office, sufficiently indicated the kind of expedition which the Department was willing to authorize. But if reports be true you will much exceed this amount, the consequences of which will be to involve yourself in the most serious difficulties.

I hear also that among other things, you have been calling upon the Ordnance Department for a Howitzer. Now Sir what authority had you to make any such requisition, and of what use can such a piece be in the execution of your duties. Where is your right to increase your party in the numbers & expense, which the management and preser-

vation of such a piece require. If the condition of the Indians in the mountains is such as to require your party to be
so warlike in its equipment it is clear that the only objects
of your expedition geographical information cannot be
obtained.

The object of the Department was a peaceable expedition,
similar to the one of last year, an expedition to gather scientific knowledge. If there is reason to believe that the
condition of the country will not admit of the safe management of such an expedition, and of course will not admit of the only objects for the accomplishment of which
the expedition was planned, you will immediately desist
in its further prosecution and report to this office.

Very Respectfully.

Your Obt. Servt.,

J. J. Abert, Col. Corps T. E.

Through the haze of institutional prose the essential point is fairly
clear: if you need the cannon, the expedition is off. When this letter
arrived in Jessie's hands in St. Louis, as she later recalls the incident, she
didn't hesitate. She held on to the letter and sent a message to her husband (up the river at Kaw Landing, now Kansas City) telling him to
leave immediately. He did. Jessie may have thought it a good idea for
her husband to have a cannon. She certainly thought that her husband
needed to go on his second expedition to the Rocky Mountains.

Eight months later, the day after John Charles abandoned his cannon in the Sierras, Secretary Porter was cleaning out his office in Washington. He had said of the matter:

This whole proceeding appears to have been singularly
irregular. If the party of the topographical corps needed
arms, they should have applied through the regular channels, and *in season*. Putting off the application to the last
hour was ill-advised, and the consequences should have
been visited upon those in fault. Order, regularity, and system, must be preserved, and the commandant of the de-

partment should not have required, and officers of the ordnance should never have issued, public property in the irregular manner in which this was done. I cannot sanction
the proceeding.

Always prefer a boss like Col. Abert, who worries about expenditures, to one who is mainly concerned with order and regulation.
Secretary Porter's appointment was a temporary one. Jessie's Papa,
Senator Thomas Benton spoke for three hours to the committee meeting in closed session to decide whether to sanction his confirmation
to the position. They could not.

As when he was born, John Charles was to arrive in the civilized
world unbeknownst of the fact that he had been involved in controversy for the better part of a year. He wouldn't again have a period of
such innocence as when he had only the winter Sierras with which to
contend, but he was always to be well-allied. They were a tough team,
Jessie and John Charles, he protected her when they were together on
the frontier, she him when they were in town. Eventually, in their old
age, she'd have to support them with her writing. But did her husband need protecting at the time she and he were writing the *Report*,
in the spring of 1845?

I made a pact with myself before coming: in situations where the
evidence was not conclusive, I would believe the story I was acting
upon. When searching the hollow for the cannon, I expected the
cannon to be there. There were clumps of brush I crawled out of
surprised not to have found the cannon in them, thinking I ought to
search again.

I hadn't so far had to exercise this willing suspension of disbelief
with regard to motives. But now that the question of Harry Tom's
motives insinuated itself into the search, and we could no longer search
only the low sides of hills with an eye to horseback height, the area to
be searched was greatly expanded. We couldn't search it all.

John Charles said they left the cannon because of the deep snow
and steep terrain. They *could* leave the cannon becausethey were out
of the region of the warlike tribes. They knew it would be tough to
get the cannon over the Sierra Nevada; they hadn't been able to get
the cannon into camp the day before—only the second time that had

happened on the expedition. To these unassailable propositions I added two probables: 1)the snow was soft on the warm days and was breakable crust on the cold days; 2)they were happy to abandon the cannon. In order to not make John Charles a liar, I mentally emended the *Report* to have meant to say: "We left it, to the great sorrow of the whole party, who—though relieved at the moment to be disencumbered of their burden—were grieved to part...etc." It is a small detail in a large report. The Congress was waiting for the report. John Charles was in the midst of preparing for that summer's expedition while writing it. The country was waiting to settle the West. Even in a report as carefully prepared as the one prepared by John Charles and Jessie, you can expect to drop a clause here and there.

What we needed to look for then was a north or east facing slope steep enough to not make the abandoning appear to have been done with unseemly haste.

One Discovery After Another

There was frost before dawn on Sunday morning, a bright moon charged the sky with pale light through which shown a bright planet in the southwest sky. We were up at 0515, underway at 0530, back for the boots I forgot at 0545 and breakfast was on the table at the Hays Street Cafe at 0620. At 0940 we were down to the 6700 foot level in the South Fork of Cottonwood Creek looking at a beaver lodge.

We had traversed from the outcropping on the south rim into the middle of the South Fork. Because the most likely place for the cannon was the lower section, and because we no longer had the authority of Harry Tom to narrow the band of terrain we searched, our plan was to search downstream to the meadow on one side of the stream and back up to our entry point on the other side, in a search line of two. You can never find a troop of boy scouts when you need them. While still some distance above the stream bed we came upon an area of fallen trees.

"Avalanche last winter?"

"Or blowdown?"

No...only the cottonwoods were down.

"Well, well—beaver! Look at these tooth marks, they look like they were made with an adz."

We worked our way down through 70 or 80 yards of fallen trunks, many over eight inches in diameter at the base, to the stream where there was a series of three dams and the lodge. The dams weren't breached but did need minor repair. The lodge was intact. It appeared that the beaver had colonized last year or, at most, the year before, but were gone. Mountain lion?

"There's your beaver sign, Kit," I thought.

I startled myself thinking of Kit Carson directly in the second person that way. He seemed present, hearing my thoughts, watching me turn my head away so that Trevor wouldn't see me smile at the thought of it. This had to do not with spirits but with veracity.

"You really were here," I thought, changing to "you" plural to include them all, "maybe not here in this fork but here someplace in this hollow—or on the rim." In that moment I stopped distrusting Fremont and his men, as if I had their acquaintance, knew them well enough to know their motives. It was the beaver sign that did it:

January 17—This morning we left the river, which here issues from the mountains on the west. With every stream I now expected to see the great Buenaventura; and Carson hurried eagerly to search, on every one we reached, for beaver cuttings, which he always maintained we should find only on waters that ran to the Pacific; and the absence of such signs was to him a sure indication that the water had no outlet from the great basin.

Kit was right. The beaver now in the drainages of the Eastern Sierra, those that made the dams and lodge before us, were introduced there. How did Carson know . . . or, what was it exactly that he did know? How did he learn it: from the Indians, other trappers, mountain man intuition? I had forgotten how much more they knew than any of us know about what a beaver is up to. I still sometimes think of persons who lived when the earth was younger as themselves childlike, as if history is just a forgotten part of my childhood. Also, not unlike child development, the fame of explorers grows by the mistakes they correct, as well as the new marvels they find. On this expedition Fremont and his men disposed of the Buenaventura River, the last youthful fantasy of the theoretical geographers.

The Buenaventura was one of the minor creations of the theoretical geographers. *Terra Australis Incognita* and the Northwest Passage are the great late examples, leading in their disproving great explorers to great discoveries: Cook to Antarctica, Australia, New Zealand, Oceana, Hawaii, Nootka Sound and Alaska; Vancouver to Puget Sound and the Columbia River. Fremont knew he was in the tradition of Cook, and probably realized that the Buenaventura was it: the last story of an undiscovered feature of the planet earth. As with Cook and Vancouver, Carson and Fremont were eagerly searching for something they had good reason to suspect doesn't exist, but all that means is that more concentration is required. Because of a minor lapse of attention, Vancouver missed the Columbia River and suffered the indignity of having to be told about it by a Yankee trader, Captain Gray of the "Columbia." A form of concentration is to believe it is there while you are looking for it.

Men like these, Carson, Fitzpatrick, Fremont, Preuss, the voyageurs, who have paid a fair price for what they know, do not involve themselves in petty deceptions, in falsifying records. Nobody was trying to fool us, we just hadn't yet figured out where the route went and where the cannon was abandoned.

We continued our search down the South Fork until we were almost to the meadow, then traversed out and into the canyon of the North Fork, just for the hell of it, and then returned to the South Fork to hike back up it to its head.

We stopped searching seriously when we got back up to the beaver sign. Did I want to look at anything else? No. Trevor—who had not been as quick to form a new hypothesis as I, realizing perhaps that, though they were not difficult to formulate, you might be living with the new hypothesis for a year—began thinking about the chart of the distances from camp to camp that Fremont had appended to the *Report*. The mileages don't quite fit anybody's notion of where the camp on the height was, giving us a wider area in which to relocate it.

I was not working on an hypothesis. I was enjoying a feeling that not only was our search over for the time, we had succeeded at finding . . . something. My Uncle Ray told me to always keep an eye out for that rare and most precious of finds, a gold-plated excuse. Maybe that was it. My sense that the principals in this game were playing fair included Lewis. What he said in his introduction was:

> My interest in the howitzer began in 1957 while visiting friends in Bridgeport, California. They could hardly wait for the coming weekend so they could go cannon hunting. My interest was piqued when they related a number of local legends concerning cannon sightings. Admittedly, they had no evidence to rely on other than the campfire stories of hunters and fishermen, but the sheer numbers of the sightings were enough to convince them that somewhere in the mountains within thirty miles of Bridgeport there was a cannon, its wooden wheels crumbling with age, its irons rusting, but with its brass barrel intact and awaiting a lucky finder. I accompanied them on their trek into the wilderness. The mountains, valleys and streams were spectacular, the air exhilarating, and the treasure search mind-boggling. Suddenly I found myself believing that the cannon was in the next grove of trees, or around the next bend or in the next canyon. The day was so spiritually uplifting it didn't matter when I found later we were forty miles from where the cannon was probably located.

It was exactly as he said. We seemed to have found a goldplated excuse for a walk in the woods. And more. It would come to me eventually. I puttered along in a manner of pleased abstraction whilst we wandered up through the canyon.

Half mile from the head of the canyon, we came on another area of fallen trees. Windfall. I decided to see how far I could get walking on the trunks and limbs, not touching the ground and not backtracking: a game I'd given up when I graduated to Explorer Scout from Boy Scout. I'd never been in better country for this game, open groves of cottonwoods, eight inch grass with wildflowers, no underbrush, no trunk more than three feet from the ground. I was doing very well—200 yards, having thoughts of making a quarter of a mile—when I got too far out on a limb and it broke. Because the trunk the limb belonged to had ended up perched on a boulder, which in turn was on the edge of the embankment of a former channel of the stream, I ended up falling about ten feet and landing on my shoulders.

"Are you okay?" Trevor asked as my breath returned.

That was, as we are wont to say in my trade, a good question: I was careless if not silly; and, had I not landed right between a rock and a sharp stick, I would have been bloody. I discontinued the game, became less abstracted, but continued pleased. I had some precedent for my foolishness. My very favorite passage in the *Report* is in the account of the first expedition. They have returned from the Wind Rivers and the first ascent of Fremont Peak and are in white water below where the Sweetwater joins the Platte:

> We cleared rock after rock, and shot past fall after fall, our little boat seeming to play with the cataract. We became flushed with success and familiar with the danger; and, yielding to the excitement of the occasion, broke forth together into a Canadian boat song. Singing, or rather shouting, we dashed along; and were, I believe, in the midst of the chorus, when the boat struck a concealed rock immediately at the foot of a fall, which whirled her over in an instant.

We returned to camp for our last evening in cannon country.

What about Harry Tom, what about his motives? I put myself in his position. The cannon on the Mono Courthouse lawn is fifty or sixty feet from the walkway to the entrance. What did Harry Tom think as he saw Ella Cain leave the sidewalk and start across the grass toward him? My guess was that Harry Tom thought, "She thinks I've seen one of these up country and don't know its value," and improvised from there. The rest is, in a manner of speaking, history. He probably began to sweat a little when she asked him for a map. If she did. The map could easily be an improvement made during the story's oral tradition. The important point is, there is hardly anything that Harry Tom could have given us that would have pleased us more than his story of seeing one of these old cannons way up in the mountains.

As Harry Tom's progenitors in the area in 1844 found out, whatever you tell the whites, they hear only what they want to hear. These pine nut eaters living in the verge were a particularly unwarlike group of Indians, who did their best to help the whites. It wasn't easy. They discovered in the whites an amazing obtuseness about what the country was telling them. A week after they abandoned the cannon, against advice they had received from every group of Indians they asked, Fremont and his men was forcing his crossing of the Sierra Nevada south of Lake Tahoe. The Indians tried once again:

February 4—....To-night we had no shelter, but we made a large fire around the trunk of one of the huge pines; and covering the snow with small boughs, on which we spread our blankets, soon made ourselves comfortable. The night was very bright and clear, though the thermometer was only at 10 degrees. A strong wind, which sprang up at sundown, made it intensely cold; and this was one of the bitterest nights during the journey.

Two Indians joined our party here; and one of them, an old man, immediately began to harangue us, saying that ourselves and animals would perish in the snow; and that if we would go back, he would show us another and a better way across the mountain. He spoke in a very loud voice, and there was a singular repetition of phrases and arrangement of words, which rendered his speech striking, and not unmusical.

We had now begun to understand some words, and, with the aid of signs, easily comprehended the old man's simple ideas. "Rock upon rock—rock upon rock—snow upon snow—snow upon snow," said he; "even if you get over the snow, you will not be able to get down from the mountains." He made us a sign of precipices, and showed us how the feet of the horses would slip, and throw them off from the narrow trails which led along their sides. Our

Chinook, who comprehended even more readily than ourselves, and believed our situation hopeless, covered his head
with his blanket, and began to weep and lament. "I wanted
to see the whites," said he; "I came away from my own
people to see the whites, and I wouldn't care to die among
them; but here"—and he looked around into the cold night
and gloomy forest, and, drawing his blanket over his head,
began again to lament.

Seated around the tree, the fire illuminating the rocks and
the tall bolls of the pines round about, and the old Indian
haranguing, we presented a group of very serious faces.

Fremont makes the most extraordinary account about what happens next:

February 5—The night had been too cold to sleep, and we were
up very early. Our guide was standing by the fire with all
his finery on; and seeing him shiver in the cold, I threw on
his shoulders one of my blankets. We missed him a few
minutes afterwards, and never saw him again. He had de-
serted. His bad faith and treachery were in perfect keeping
with the estimate of Indian character, which a long inter-
course with this people had gradually forced upon my mind.

Their guide was a young man named Melo, meaning friend. When
John Charles threw his blanket over his shoulder, Melo must have been
terrified. Melo had probably come to think of his elders' orders to
accompany the whites as a sentence of death. That the whites would
also die would not have cheered him any more than it cheered the
Chinook they had brought with them. It was terrifying to be among
these insane people determined to kill themselves. Melo probably no
longer cared to try to figure out why they wanted to kill themselves.
They said they wanted to see the other whites across the mountains.
That couldn't be the real reason. They would have gone to the south if
it were. It was probably some unfathomable spirit thing, one cannot
easily know about that of a distant people. Melo probably did have
some interest in when he was going to die, that sort of thought comes

and goes. But he must have been puzzled as to why he needed to die with them. Where was his mistake? If he hadn't talked to the other whites, he wouldn't be here. That's what comes of being too curious. What really was unfathomable was the white chief's covering his shoulders with a blanket. This act of kindness by the man who was determined to kill them all must have made the hair rise and the skin crawl on the back of his neck. What were these people! Then, his head cleared, he realized that this blanket might enable him to survive the deep snow that covered the first ten of the twenty-six miles he had to go to reach home. He probably made as if to relieve himself—and bolted.

We awoke at 0528 and were decamped and on the road by 0602. Did I want to take another look for anything, there was plenty of time? No, but I did want a last breakfast at the Hays Street Cafe.

"We thought you had left because you weren't the first ones in here this morning," said the waitress.

We stalled over breakfast in order to listen to a story being told by a man named Tom at the table to the north of us. With him were another man and Tom's eight or nine year old son. Tom was telling the story to the husband of the waitress, who was sitting at the table east of us—so we weren't really eavesdropping. Tom was wearing a Levi shirt with the sleeves cut off at the shoulder, and, strapped over his dusty logging boots, leather leggings that ran up to his knees. He was no longer a young man and not yet middle aged, talking about when he was a younger, and a wilder, man. He seemed not to regret that he was no longer that man. His story was about twice disarming men shooting up a bar. On the second occasion, two of his friends had been hit and he "got splinters all in my ear and the side of my face. My face was all bloody." After that he "went straight."

"I survived one war, I don't need to try to survive another one," he said.

But his resolution wasn't enough. Tom owned an 1881 Colt 44 that was stolen by an acquaintance, a man who had been in the country for a while, working around at this and that. He used Tom's gun to kill two people who picked him up hitch-hiking. The detectives got to the killer through Tom who they had tracked through the gun. "He was crazy, I knew he was. He got off on a civil rights violation you know, because he was put on death row before he was put on trial in Las Vegas." What Tom objected to most besides the risk was, "You can spend four years in court with one of these. I lost a lot of work, couldn't count on doing anything, people couldn't count on me being able to be there all the time."

As if reminded by that, he got up and left. His son had scarcely wiggled in his chair during the time his Daddy was talking. Out the window I watched them go to toward the cab of a stake-bed truck, chainsaw, peavey, and rope cable in the bed of it, the boy lined up behind his Daddy, matching his long swinging stride as precisely as the length of his legs would allow.

When I got back home my wife told me about a conversation she had with our youngest daughter who was seventeen. When she was twelve, we got her a horse, a thoroughbred recently off the track and gelded proud. She had learned physical courage domesticating that horse, and moral courage. While her friends were winning ribbons in 4H shows, she was trying to keep the horse from hurting somebody. Eventually the horse turned into a pretty decent critter. The conversation my wife and daughter were having was about what to do about the horse while she was away at college. Connie said she'd keep the horse in shape for her. Summer replied in calm seriousness that it didn't really matter because after college there would be work and it was unlikely that the world would last long enough for her ever to get to ride her horse again after she leaves home. Connie was really taken aback, by her matter-of-factness more than her view of her prospects. I wished to tell her about how we look for the Northwest Passage, and *Terra Australis Incognita*, and the Buenaventura, and lost cannons, and world peace, or just one more day as good as one you once remember having—and the trick of believing we will find them when we have good reasons to believe we won't. And when that doesn't work, how to shout a song when shooting the rapids.

I came back in January to be where they had been on the 143rd anniversary of their being there. I traveled to Bridgeport by Greyhound Bus so that I would have to walk up to the pass and could not be tempted to drive up. They were mounted but I had 395 so I figured it was about even.

I couldn't go out on the reconnaissance day because my pack had gotten on another bus. I didn't mind, a day at altitude wouldn't hurt and the Hays Street Cafe was still in business for breakfast and lunch and doing well. Also it was Superbowl Sunday and there was a big gathering at the Bodie Mining Company Inn. I hiked in the next day, every sense remembering the winter I worked as a cowhand in Jackson Hole: the green of the hay on the snow, the aggrieved bawling of the cows, their perfume, the heat of the work in the cold air, and the sweet taste of that air. The best of it all was checking the herd at midnight. We didn't have to do anything but check: the sleeping forms lifting their heads as the horse picked his way through, the coyotes taking over the night with their calling from the hillsides, the black sky quaking with stars. No subsequent job has put me as much at peace with the world.

Trevor flew down to L.A. and Michael and he showed up on the Fremont Carson Route on the 28th. They got Michael's pickup in a mile before getting stuck. I came down from the ridges where I had been making large circuits, certain that Fremont's men hadn't gone to the very highest ridges, not with a cannon.

The three of us snowshoed into the hollow. We stopped below the north rim of the hollow and on the east side of 8422 to listen to a magpie yell at us. The magpie stopped and there was a startlingly loud noise. The noise was the sound of a snowshoe shifted in the crusty snow. I asked Michael and Trevor to hold still. There was no sound. None. No wind, no stream, no river, no engines of car or plane. We may never have that experience again. On the way back there was the track of the cougar.

I now knew what we found in cannon country. I saw it in June without recognizing it.

High up on the road to Sonora Pass, well into the timber, we stopped to look back at cannon country a little below us. It was indeed in the verge: below the timber, too high to irrigate for hay and pasture. Deer thrived there, we'd seen dozens; we'd started a coyote out of its noonday nap just the day before. It wasn't wilderness. There had been sheep grazing there at one time; we had found Basque names and fifty year old dates carved in the cottonwoods. There were old mines higher up. Nevertheless, the country had been spared much use by people. It was essentially as it had been. That's what we found, the land as it was. If we could just find that cannon, those 143 years would vanish.

Kit would say to Fitzpatrick, "Remember how tough we thought it was here? And this weren't nothin'?"

Fitzpatrick would say, "Didn't we get hongry and tired of snow-banks afore we got to Sutter's!"

And I, no longer caring whether they were happy or sad to have been relieved of their cannon, would say, "Tell me about the time the mule ate Fitzpatrick's saddle."

And it would be a story worth remembering.

A Dozen Years Afterword

It was three-quarters of the way through January and raining in Olym-pia. No surprise that; the surprise is that after a quarter century of Pacific Northwest Januarys they can still get to me. I was team-teach-ing, in a coordinated studies program with a folklorist and a natural-ist. It was titled Re-storying the West, which of course everybody heard as "restoring the West." Again, not a surprise. You can't expect everybody to have read Barry Lopez—unless you're feeling grumpy.

If a change is needed ain't nobody but you to do something about it. The Super Bowl was coming up. So was the 152nd anniversary of Fremont's trek across Devil's Gate, and the tenth anniversary of the most fun I ever had at watching a football game. That was at the bar in Bridgeport, California. I called the motor pool. They had a van. I told my seminar that they were invited to join me in searching for the canon, we'd be leaving in three days. About half joined me. I hadn't told them about the Super-Bowl. They'd have to earn that.

Down the road we went. South to and then east along the Colum-bia River. Once we got through the Gorge, the Cascades dropping behind us, the rain stopped. The clouds were climbing over the Cas-cades in pursuit. I refused to turn south until we had a comfortable lead on the clouds. No going the short way down 97 this time.

How about Blalock? Oops, past it before I could make up my mind. Arlington then, due south to Fossil where we could jog over to 395, the favorite highway of my friends who are naturalists or poets. Highway 395 starts in Laurier, which would be in the middle of nowhere except that you can't really call a town on an international border in the middle of nowhere. From Laurier the road accompanies the Kettle River 11 miles down to Orient, Washington then 11 more miles to Boyds, no apostrophe, then 10 miles to Kettle Falls, crossing the Columbia River just out of town, and 10 miles to Coleville and the Coleville River. Then 395 forgets what it is all about and wanders into Spokane, whereupon it is gobbled up by I 90 for sixty miles, escapes for seventy-five miles, is recaptured by I 82 in Washington and I 84 in Oregon pushes it east from Hermiston to Pendleton, where 395 determinedly heads south securely in the middle of nowhere until it gets to Reno. From Reno 395 nestles up against the Sierra Nevada, runs down the spectacular east side through California's most beautiful and least populated counties. When the Sierra peters out, 395 is sucked westward into the Los Angeles vortex and total annihilation. We would stop in Cannon Country before we got that far.

At dark we were rounding Malheur Lake on 78, having turned east at Burns Junction, headed for 95. We hit it within an hour's drive from the Mountain Time Zone at the Idaho border. We'd dodged the storm all day. Now we would have to take it head-on in the dark. There was snow on the mountaintops and ice on Blue Mountain Pass. Then there was freezing rain and terrifying traffic on I 80. Fortunately we were only a hundred miles and change from Reno. I was wondering if I might not be able to uncurl my hands from the wheel.

Raining hard in Reno. I couldn't get out of the van. Around and around I drove, looking for a motel that is cheap enough, clean enough and close enough. There it was, The Shamrock, I knew what I was looking for when I found it. It was after midnight, about 90 minutes after midnight. Could I rouse the clerk? What was I thinking? This is Reno we are talking about! The clerk got to the desk from the dark room behind before I get to it from the front. He is a kindly Mexican about my age. I made it. Home for the night.

There are nine of us. Probably we need two rooms? We can sleep on the floor. We have sleeping bags.

You have sleeping bags? Oh, that's good. You can have the suite for seventy-two dollars.

Wonderful!

Five students piled out of the room into town. When they returned, I awoke enough to hear them joshing Jen, who is wont to complain that she likes men more than they like her, accusing her of bedazzling a young waiter and then cruelly dashing his hopes. I went back to sleep smiling at one of the rare rewards of not being young.

We made an easy day of the next day. They were given a liberal amount of time to wander the streets of Virginia City. I told them that this was part of cannon hunting because Mark Twain made Virginia City famous. They didn't bat an eyelash. After fourteen weeks in my seminar they were used to me answering a question other than the one they asked, and answering questions they had not asked. At first they think I'm just a contrary Yankee, or a selfish one, keeping his knowledge, hoarding it so he will have more than they. After twelve years of schooling, it is hard for them to adopt the notion that thinking is more important than right answers. They do learn eventually, but not without discomfort. In the first week of seminar, the first time someone breaks a silence for that reason alone, I say, "It's okay to think in seminar."

Back down in the Basin, I broke out Fremont's journal. Lyra read the parts about where we are, what he and his men were doing when they were there where we were. I didn't tell them that some day I am going to have to do this on foot. I didn't tell them to imagine seeing this for the first time. I didn't tell them to imagine being here not knowing for sure that these rivers do not go to the ocean. You don't want to take over a young person's imagination for them.

We camped outside of Yerington in an abandoned dump next to an open pit mine. There was the sound of machinery and the glow on the tailings above us of powerful lights in the pit.

A flood of the West Walker River the previous month had completely destroyed 395 in the canyon below the Fremont-Carson Road. We had to get into Bridgeport via the pass north from Mono Lake.

We approached in snow showers, but Bridgeport was sunglasses bright with snow and blue sky. Without stopping I went through town and up to a snowed-in campground just below Devil's Pass. The snow there was about 30 inches on the level. We began digging out a place for the fifteen passenger van, working hard to set up our camp before dark. We were almost through when the California Highway Patrolman cruised slowly by us and pulled over in front of us.

Years ago the college adopted the practice of not printing our name and logo on the sides of the vans in ten inch, bright green letters. Instead they paste a 5"x7" transparent decal with dark 3/8" letters on the smoked glass of the back window—right under a rung of the roof rack ladder. So the vans are anonymous, but greeners of all vintages dress like the greeners of the first vintage of 1971. The greeners of the first vintage dressed as they had a couple of years earlier in the sixties. To complete the ensemble, my shoulder-length gray hair was not in a ponytail.

As I feared, he wanted to know what we were doing, more than who we were. When I said what there was no escaping saying, that we were looking for John Charles Fremont's lost cannon, the patrolman turned his head away, and then down at the side of his boot.

Silence. Then he lifted his head and rolled his eyes almost to the Sierra summits. Wondering, I was sure, just how much and what kind of sarcasm was warranted by the occasion.

Did I ever misread Bob McColloch. He smiled a big smile and began:

> Somewhere tucked in a nearby canyon
> Is old Captain Fremont's 500 pound cannon.
> He had to give it up in 1844
> For his men couldn't push it anymore.

He'd forgotten some of the words of his next stanza. Bob had hooked me with his rhyme of "push it anymore" with "1844." I had to have the rest of it. He agreed to bring it by the next day.

We snow-shoed up to the base of good old 8422, no cougar tracks this time, and headed back in time enough to go into town for the Super Bowl. We'd had to park the van a couple of miles down the road at the junction. Dave, who didn't have snowshoes, was with the van. I was back, sweeping the hill of stragglers, so to speak, so when I got to the road they had asked a Deputy County Sheriff, who had come by, to tell Dave that we were ready to go. Dave got talking with the deputy and told him what we were doing. The Deputy came back up the road just minutes after I arrived.

"He's on his way," he said, and then added, shaking his finger at me, "I want you to know that that is my cannon!" and went on down the road. Apparently all the law enforcement officers in Mono County were cannon hunters!

During halftime of the Super Bowl, seven of us won prizes in the raffle. Mine was a fifth of Metaxa.

Every hunt begins with a story of where cannon must be. And so far, every hunt ends with another story about why the cannon wasn't found this time. There are basically two kinds of these after-hunt stories, depending on whether you want to continue the hunt or not. If you don't, you tell a story like the cannon was melted down during the Civil War. Bob McColloch has a real good story. He says, "I think that one of these big ranchers around here probably found the cannon years ago and it's tucked away in some old barn with old cars and the horse drawn hay rakes." Think about it. There's nothing wrong with hunting for the cannon just in case that story isn't true. On the other hand, if it *is* true, the cannon is still there. Here's the rest of Bob's poem:

> People have searched for it all around
> They talk about it at the bars in town.
> But so far, it has stayed well hid
> That is until I make my bid.
>
> Someday I plan to take my horse
> And follow old Fremont's wandering course.
> I'll ride around, looking under every tree
> And anywhere else that cannon may be.
>
> I know at last, I'll find it some way
> Oh how that will be a happy day.
> I can picture that cannon in my mind

Right there where Fremont left it behind.
When I find it I'll probably be forced
To drag it behind my trusty old horse.
But I know it will be worth the work so hard
To have that cannon displayed
In my own front yard.

What's gold compared to a fine story of hope like that?

Smoke and Remembrance

Finding the Fire

At noon on the day the Yellowstone fire reached 1,000,000 acres destroyed (as they had been saying in the papers, though of course the acres were still there), I ate lunch in the privacy of a thicket of naturally bonzaied spruce at 10,025 feet on the north side of Mount Washburn. Below me roiling smoke silently swept from view the lower slopes of the mountain, and, for that matter, all of northwestern Wyoming. On the ridge two hundred yards to the west of me were three fire fighters from the U.S. Forest Service, their gear piled at the side of the dirt road to the summit of the mountain. With the gear was one of the white rental cars being used to supplement the fleets of all manner of official vehicles cruising the park. Why white I couldn't imagine. Are there a lot of them in the lots because white is the color business travelers never choose? I could catch the tone only of a desultory conversation carried on by hand-held radio with someone down in the smoke, possibly in Canyon Junction or Tower Falls, or with fire fighters working on the fire below the ridge up west of Dunraven Pass. I could see the guy with the radio, but, because of the thicket, they could not see me. I did not want to bother them.

I had a similar reluctance to disturb the folks in the fire tower that capped the mountain. The shoulder of the summit blocked my view of all but the tops of the antennas protruding from the roof of the structure. Given the conditions then prevailing, these antennae were undoubtedly their principal organs of perception; but for the crest of the hill, I would have been what there was to see besides smoke. I moved anxiously from the thicket to the road where. Keeping to the inside of the road, I continued not bothering the folks on the ridge or in the tower. I paused fifty feet short of the southwest shoulder at a gully that, in crossing, would put me in full view of the tower. I sat down.

The promised southwest wind, two hours late, began to stir massive banks of gray smoke to the south and east, not taking it anywhere, just churning it. All the places to put smoke were full.

To the west, from torching trees, trees whose crowns catch fire almost instantaneously, fresh white columns of steam towered out of the gray mass of older smoke—surprising that there could be, at the end of this summer, water enough left in the trees to make steam. The fire was coming down the crest of the ridge on the other side of Dunraven Pass toward me: the columns rising in sequence west to east as if a rack of bombs had been dropped. It would be nice to have a look at what was happening down in the pass itself. The road might have been closed, but it wasn't officially closed to me until there was an official there to tell me. I had to go through Dunraven Pass to get to the South Entrance, or I'd be not a hundred and thirty miles from Jackson, but five hundred. Risk being seen or risk driving for eight or ten more hours?

The first smoke I saw of the 1988 fire season was from Chinook Pass, a dozen air miles east of the summit of Mt. Rainier. The temperature in Seattle that day was 98, breaking the old record for that date by 7 degrees. I was driving to Jackson, Wyoming to be with my oldest daughter, Melanie, at the birth of my first grandchild—via Pullman, where my youngest daughter, Summer, had just started college. Son Kirk was already in Jackson hiking, climbing, and fishing with Larry, a neighbor of ours.

The smoke got thicker as I approached Pullman, except that the air was nearly clear over the Hanford Nuclear Reservation, as if the emanations from that facility were of sufficient potency to render mere smoke invisible. In Pullman I dropped off some zucchini bread from mother, and chatted for a bit with Summer's computer until it revealed to us how the printer wished to be bespoke. At the crest of the Lewiston Hill, I learned from one of the two signs there that Idaho Territory was proclaimed in Lewiston July 10, 1863 and the first two legislatures met in Lewiston, Idaho Territory (then including what is now modern Montana, while most of Wyoming was attached to Dakota). Then the governor and legislature decided to locate the capital of Idaho in Boise, where it has been ever since. The other sign issued a cautious invitation:

> When automobile traffic made steep old wagon roads obsolete, a remarkable new highway grade was built down this hill in 1917. With a series of sharp curves that let cars go 20 or 30 miles an hour—a good speed for that time—a gradual 10-mile 2000 foot grade was designed. It can still be used by anyone not in too much of a hurry who wants to see an engineering model of early highway construction.

First babies are usually late, so I went down the remarkable grade at the 1917 speed, but it wasn't engineering, steepness then vs. steepness now, or rolls-to-the-bottom that I had on my mind. What had impressed me is that from the top of the hill I could see only one bend in the Snake River before it disappeared, as did the Clearwater River, and the far sides of the towns of Lewiston and Clarkston. By the time I got to the bottom of the grade, I realized that I was immersed in a natural phenomenon of amazing proportions. The debate I'd been reading in the *Jackson Hole News*—about whether this was a natural or an unnatural phenomenon, whether it was unnatural to fight the fires or unnatural not to, and who could be held accountable—seemed a little silly. It took a sense of self-importance larger than any I'd been able to muster since I was three years old to assume responsibility for a dense bank/cloud of smoke that extended from the Cascades eastward to the Rockies and beyond, a distance greater than that from New York to Chicago, covering possibly all of the old Oregon, Idaho, and Dakota Territories.

I was mightily impressed. I planned to take Highway 12 over Lolo Pass. When Melanie was a young girl, and I was a graduate student at the University of Washington in the winter and a park ranger and then a mountain guide in the summer, we traveled from Puget Sound to Jackson Hole and back twice a year, there in June, return to Seattle in September and out and back at Christmas. Usually we, Connie, Melanie, Kirk, me and our dog Jenny Leigh evenly distributed in our VW Bug, went south to the Columbia River and up it as far as the Umatilla Wildlife Refuge, across Northeastern Oregon to the Snake River and up it to Jackson. If we had decent weather and time, we took the northern route via Spokane to Missoula and then from there either on to Yellowstone or south through Salmon and then east to enter the valley over Teton Pass. Only once had we used Lolo Pass. Highway 12 is much slower: more curves, steeper grades and narrow lanes and, with 128 miles between gas stations, it was an adventure. We could thinking of ourselves as driving right through the wilderness.

There is now gas available at the Lochsa Lodge, near the summit of the pass. Nonetheless, the fires kept enough of the old sense of adventure alive that when I got to the Ranger Station at Kooskia, still open at 6 p.m. on a Saturday evening, I decided to stop in to hear what they could say about the fires. There were two women in the station. The one at the information desk told me that none of the fires were near the road and all but the two campgrounds nearest the summit were open. The other woman, on the phone at a working desk, was involved in the logistics of fire fighting. "We've got to get those men up there," she said. "Up where?" I wondered. But since they were probably open only because of the fires, and I knew from experience that talking to tourists was work, I went on my way. I camped that night where the road started its climb up the pass.

The first fire camp was only four hundred feet from the highway in a meadow near the White Sand Campground a few miles west of the pass. That's why the high campgrounds were closed. The fire camp, about the size of a platoon, had the look of an encampment of military irregulars. I felt the urge again to talk to someone fighting these fires but kept on. Just past the entrance to the campground, a young woman was tacking up a temporary sign. A forest service pick-up was parked beside the road. I glanced in my rear view mirror to see if

I could read the sign, but her truck blocked my view.

Slowly, hesitantly I drove on, feeling like I was missing my main chance. I should not be passing this by. In this, the fire season of the century, I had thus far seen smoke and read letters to the editor. I had fought wildfires, I wasn't wanting that, my time for digging fire lines was past. Why I believed I was entitled to more than what the walls of flame we had seen on television provided I don't know. Perhaps I felt that my many memories of my time in the mountains earned me a perspective, some sense of what it all meant. Perspective means direct experience. Experience of what? The camera man filming the wall of flames? First there's the film, later there's the film about making the film.

I'd be at the monthly poker game with my buddies.

"So you were there, in Yellowstone?"

"Yup, up around Lewis Lake it was, you know the headwaters of the Snake—and the Columbia. The CNN crew were way ahead of the ABC guys. I saw one guy with burn holes in his Filson field vest and his hundred dollar Akubra hat. Flesh wounds to the raiment."

I continued in a state of unease until I came upon a sign, not there when I last passed this way, "DeVoto Memorial Cedar Grove." A scholar, a kindred soul! I stopped to read:

> This majestic grove of Western Red Cedar is dedicated
> to the memory of Bernard DeVoto, conservationist, au-
> thor, and historian. He often camped here while studying
> the journals of Lewis and Clark. At his request his ashes
> were scattered over this area.

DeVoto was all the added authority I needed. I turned around and drove back to the sign that the young woman tacked up, "fire information ahead." God rest your soul for your intercession Bernard DeVoto, I'll have my students read both, "Across the Wide Missouri" and "The Journals of Lewis and Clark." Your heirs will be wealthy.

Her pick-up half-blocked traffic to and from the fire camp. Her truck was on the out-going not the in-going side. Already I was impressed with her ability to handle us rubber-necking folks. Elbow out the window I stopped abreast of her, driver to driver. Shandra is from

Hawaii. Though now in the Forest Service, she started out in the Park Service, at the Arizona Memorial, and then to the Coulee National Monument. When she had enough of visitors—as we are known to park ranger—she decided to find some woods and animals other than us. The fire fighters came from everywhere she said, as was impressed upon her when the group from Georgia arrived. I mentioned that 2500 fire fighters had been sent to Yellowstone from our neighborhood, Fort Lewis, with, we were told, ten hours of training. Shandra said yes, she had had that sort of training in the Park Service. The Forest Service training was 35 hours, with annual renewal. A pickup turned off the highway and stopped behind me. I moved behind her, engine idling so she'd know I wasn't staying. I remembered being on her side of conversations where the person is making up reasons to talk to you because you are to them the real Smokey the Bear. When the guys in the pickup got their fair share of information and unblocked the road, I pulled out, waving and calling thanks to Shandra, and headed for the pass.

There was another fire camp at the bottom of the Montana side of the pass, right beside the road. It too had an information vehicle at the entrance but I wasn't tempted. Here is where I had to choose to go south or east. I remembered that the smoke jumpers were headquartered at the airfield west of Missoula. They would know whether Yellowstone would be closed or not. My information from the Jackson paper was two weeks old. Also, a buddy of mine used to fly for them and had often said I should stop. Now I had an adequate reason to get a glimpse of life as a smokejumper. I signed-up for the airborne and OCS in the Army and made the wrong choice. Had I chose the airborne I would have acquired a useable skill.

It turns out I didn't need a good reason, they expect company. At the entrance to the Aerial Fire Depot, as it is termed, there was both a trailer with a table for checking in incoming firefighters and a visitor's center, with film strips, murals including the complete interior of a fire tower that had once been out in the forest, an information desk manned by a man and a woman who looked to be retired volunteers, and a sign above the desk announcing tours of the facility on the hour.

I asked if they knew if Yellowstone was closed.

"Well it hasn't been, but judging by what was in the paper this morning, I would think so," she said.

"What happened? I've been driving and I haven't seen a paper yet."

"Well, they're evacuating West Yellowstone and Cooke City."

"That's the West Entrance and the Northeast Entrance, and I know that the South Entrance has been closed for some time. Do you think I could go in the North Entrance and out by the East Entrance?"

"I don't know," she said doubtfully, "things are getting pretty bad. You can ask them out at the dispatch trailer."

"I'd go ahead and try it," said Robert Redford who had just entered from the back door wearing olive drab fire-resistant pants and the expensively practical logger boots, hand-made by White, that smokejumpers wear. Cowboy boots are worn in New York, Tokyo, even Paris. White boots are too expensive and too homely to be worn anywhere except in earnest. Like cowboy boots, White boots have high heels, only thicker, with a graceful, but all business, recurve like that of the cooling tower of a nuclear power plant. Wearing White boots, Wayne Williams looked exactly like Robert Redford.

"You would go ahead and try it?" I grinned, trying to remember if it was Robert Redford or Paul Newman who jumped first. "Sure, the South Entrance isn't closed, or it wasn't this morning. It was only closed for a couple of days. They close a road here and a road there but they don't close the park. Wait, I'll find out," he said darting down a stairwell. He returned in a moment with a 3" thick loose-leaf binder that contained the daily reports for every fire in the region, maybe several regions. Wayne Williams turned out to have come to the Visitor's Center to lead the tour. Or, he explained, he would lead us unless he got called out on the next fire.

I ended up taking the tour three times, once that afternoon, and twice the next day. If I hadn't begun to feel like a pest, I would have taken the tour a fourth time.

After the first tour, I drove back to Missoula feeling, for the second time that day, that I was missing something. I drove slowly around the town, stopped for coffee, drove over to the university and remembered it was Sunday, drifted back to the south of town along the road I came in on, eyeing motels, finally noted that nearly three hours had passed, time enough to have gotten to the North Entrance to Yellowstone, and accepted the fact that I was staying in Missoula that night.

My puzzlement was general, had more to do with me than with the Aerial Fire Depot—had started before I even saw the place—but it did have a focus at the Aerial Fire Depot and in Wayne Williams: what was the public relations purpose of conducting these tours? Wayne said that he wanted us to sign the visitor's book so that they would continue being included in the budget. That was puzzling. Congress would have to add millions and millions to fire-suppression this year. They don't have any choice, haven't had since 1911 when we decided that no fire that we could get men to would go unfought. The let burn procedures in the wilderness areas went into effect in 1972, but those had been abandoned almost two months ago. There should be money to burn.

We have become cynical about public relations, reading it as either public deception or self-protection from the too-knowing public. That's why they have taken to calling them "information offices." Now we watch for what is being held out of information "released" to us. That very morning Shandra, with information alone, had barred us from the fire camps. It worked because information, more than nature, is the product that the recreational managers of public lands purvey. As a ranger I sometimes dispensed information to the point of social exhaustion. I believed that information gave better access to the experience the visitor came to the park to have: camping, hiking, climbing or seeing their first moose or pine marten. Visitors eventually learned to like the experience of getting information, verbal slides as mementoes of their trip. A nature walk in the morning with a naturalist. A visit to the museum or ranger station in midday. A slide show and talk in the evening. Messing around in your campsite and schmoozing with the neighbors with the distant license plate in the meantime. With a nap and a shower in the afternoon, you could spend your allotted ten days at Jenny Lake and never tramp a poesy. It's taken me a long time to catch-on.

When I returned for my second tour, I arrived just in time to see one of the De Haviland Otters take to the air with, as it turned out, Wayne in it. Cindy, wife of one of the smoke jumpers, hair still wet from the shower, led that tour. Before we finished with her tour, the jump plane returned. They hadn't jumped because the smoke was so thick they couldn't see the ground. As a rule, they don't jump if there is too much smoke for them to see where they are going to land. Seems like a sound principle, if you can't look, don't leap.

The tour begins with the guide introducing themselves and getting their group to do the same, while strolling toward the tarmac. There we paused to look at the airplanes, specially fitted De Haviland Twin Otters, a DC-6 cargo plane, so used, and a Neptune P2V, a Navy torpedo plane converted to use for dumping 2500 gallons of fire retardant slurry on fires (gelatinous phosphate, pink, "looks like a McDonald's milkshake" but is a fertilizer). It cost about three bucks a gallon, "used to be green until they realized they needed to see where they had dumped it."

Effective?

"It doesn't do any harm, unlike borate, which we used to use. It's fertilizer, helps in the right conditions.

"No you can't put a fire out with it alone."

The Ready Room is at the far end of a building with a tower in it. What's ready are the shelves full of packed main and reserve chutes, on one side, and the jumpsuits lining the walls of the rest of the room. There is thrashing around room in there—room for eight or ten jumpers to don their jumpsuits, main and reserve parachutes, grab a personal pack, and clamber out onto the tarmac. The lockers are familiar to anyone who has lived in a barracks. The military decor is continued in the olive drab of the chute packs. The military theme seems more tolerated than aspired to. The bright yellow jump suits, personal touches and insignia on and about the lockers put one in mind of the locker room of a semi-professional sports team with high morale operating on just enough money. On both tours Wayne remarked, "this is not like a government operation," and pointed out that the military in fact picked up tips from them and not the reverse. In June of 1940, the first official year of operation for the smokejumpers, Major William Cary Lee, later to become the first Chief of the Airborne Command, visited the parachute training camp in Missoula for instruction in paratroop training, which he employed at Fort Benning, Georgia.

In the hallway right in the middle of the building, there is on one wall a display of a jumpsuit and photographs of jumping and on the opposite wall photographs of smokejumper training. This place and the cargo room, where there is a display of the tools, gear, and equipment that are dropped in with the smokejumpers are the places on the tour that are made for visitors. They are rooms full of pure information. These formal information places, and the fact that the tour does not visit the dorms, kept us from intruding while retaining the authenticity of walking and talking our way through their work place.

The manufacturing room seemed Wayne's favorite. The manufacturing room was where the smokejumpers designed and made gear like the personal pack they jumped with, or their "out of region bags," the duffel bag they take when they are sent to a more active fire region than Region One happens to be at that moment. I got the feeling that Wayne might be trying to persuade us of something in the manufacturing room. On the second tour with him I saw that he was trying to tell his story without bragging. Cindy's favorite may have been the ready room, where with its personalized lockers, there is a sign of nearly every person in her community. It was my favorite room.

The tour at the Aerial Fire Depot has exactly the right balance of formal and informal and a theme that keeps the tour guides interested in telling the story. Like most of us who have been around for a while, I have come to think of myself as a much better than average judge of character. I not imagine Wayne with a hidden agenda. Not even when he told me that he did public relations work.

Wayne looked at me askance when I lined up to take the tour a third time. Taking the tour a third time needs accounting for, I could see that. I explained that I was attracted to what they did because I once had a life that theirs reminded me of, that I was now a college professor with an interest in the authority of experience, and that I sometimes wrote about examples of it. In return for my owning-up, Wayne gave me a Forest Service monograph, "History of Smokejumping," which I assume he had a hand in writing, and, when I asked him about what he did in the winter, fessed-up to being a writer too.

So we went around again—the amateur journalist in tour with the semi-pro PR man. There is both a story to be told on the tour and a story to be made, the story that the tour itself is to become. Here's how it goes.

Facts and statistics are one basis for the tour guide's authority. Experience is the other. What good tour guides do is to use their authority to make a story that he or she and the participants work out together. It's all done by indirections. The tour guide leads with a bit of information, the number of gallons the air tanker carries. Not what we turned off the highway to find out, we then realize. Some things we can't admit to wanting to know. What is it like to watch one of your buddies auger in? So the tour guide offers up a bit of information, somebody in the group responds with a question. The tour guide answers that question and may also answer the unstated question or set up another question.

"These chutes are repacked every 90 days."

"Why?"

"It's a practice I think left over from the days of silk."

"What are the chances of both the main chute and the reserve chute not opening?"

"It's never happened in the twelve years I've been here. The serious injuries don't come from jumping—a sprained ankle now and then—but from falling trees. The DC 3 is now picking up a smokejumper who's been in the hospital since mid-July. He really got hurt bad by a tree he was felling." (When the injured smokejumper arrived he deplaned with difficulty, hospital pale, walked slowly in four inch steps, and responded to shouted greetings all around with an enormous grin. The Aerial Fire Depot was clearly the best place for him to convalesce. Talk about adding credibility to a story.)

Wayne's pride in the manufacturing room was in the innovations made over the years in that room, the gear made there in use throughout the service. Inventing and making by hand new gear is what the smokejumpers do while they wait for fires. This room is practical, this is how taxpayers get their money's worth. This is a place where people get so interested in their projects that they work on them on their own time.

The manufacturing room's easy-going spirit may also be due to the fact that it is not one of the places where they are making sure that the parachutes always open. Its utility is of a relaxed sort, the kind that we non-heroes also experience.

Is this something I could do, could have done? Are smokejumpers mainly young males trying to prove their manhood? There are only a few women smokejumpers, but that's because of the weight-carrying requirement. Most of the women who wash out do so on the last phase of a test that new and returning smokejumpers take annually. In that test they jump, work all night digging a fire line, and carry everything out several miles over rough terrain in the morning. About fifty percent wash out, most of them, men and women, do so because of the carry out. "Isn't that right Kim?" Wayne said on the first tour to the five foot five, 125 pound smokejumper. She smiled. Wayne told us the story.

"I jumped with Kim when she did that part of the test. It was not an easy carry-out. Everybody wanted our packs weighed. Mine was 110 pounds. Hers was 111. I said, 'Of course. With my experience did you think I was going to carry any extra weight?'" If that implies no sign of chauvinism at the Aerial Fire Depot, you shold know that certain of the men were proud that they could sew better than the women.

The story that I liked most was that one of the master riggers had two years earlier retired from smokejumping at age 55. The political story of the Aerial Fire Depot as an institution is that there are now 70 smokejumpers there in Missoula, down from 140 when Wayne started, down from 327 total in the nation in 1984, the year the 100,000th fire jump was made. To have become a smokejumper I would have first been part of a hotshot firefighting team, which is likely to have taken at least three years, and met certain athletic requirements: seven pull-ups, twenty-five push-ups, run a seven-and-a-half-minute mile, and carried a hundred plus pounds out after working all night. Once qualified, I would have been stationed at Missoula, at one of a half dozen subbases, or at the satellite base at West Yellowstone. If it is a light fire season where I am stationed, I will be sent somewhere else, possibly as far as Florida, California, or Alaska. When I jump, I am in a crew of eight or ten, because that is what the planes are rigged for, but my team could be as few as two. When the fire season blows up, and all the work is on the suppression of large fires, I train and serve as crew boss for pickup firefighters, serving as "overhead" (administrators of various kinds—I love the ambiguity of that term), or work as fire cache transport drivers.

Would it be worth it to me and my nation? That depends on what I understand that to mean in terms of firefighting. I'd be as effective as helicopters dipping buckets of water out of a lake. I wouldn't be as effective as the plane full of fire suppressant that happened to fly over a small town with a burning building. They dumped the whole load right on it and snuffed that house fire out like a birthday candle. Must have been a great feeling. On the average, I would jump on a fire, spend two and a half days on it and walk out carrying everything, including the stuff dropped to us in Splat Packs. If I am lucky enough to have jumped into a wilderness area, the saw I will be carrying out will not be a chainsaw but an old fashioned misery whip. Effective or not in that day's work as I see it, I would return to my base, clean up, go to a certain favorite place for a few beers, make jokes, and tell stories I hope to hear over and over again in the years ahead. According to at least one set of values we Americans sometimes honor, I would be a member of the most truly privileged class.

The stop in Missoula was well worth the price of the motel. I got to see the warriors getting ready for battle and to imagine a possible past, the same story Homer gives us in the *Iliad*. Shandra's job was to prevent that; the Aerial Fire Depot provides it to the benefit of both visitor and agency.

Firefighters were as omnipresent as smoke in Gardiner and Mammoth. I turned east out of Mammoth, headed up along the Yellowstone River, so as to position myself to exit by the East Entrance, in case all the other exits closed or got blocked by the fire. The smoke lifted off of ground level during the day, to hang in the sky above the tops of the hills, and would lower again at night. Just east of Mt. Everts, I stopped at a roadside turnout to join three people looking north at the southern edge of the Hellroaring Fire. We silently watched a single burning tree on the crest of a ridge across the valley. Another car stopped and two more people joined us. "This is the first time we have seen the actual fire," mused one, and the rest of us murmured agreement. Nothing else was said.

What is the actual fire? was the question of the summer. Skeptical of journalists, on TV or in the papers, most of us are well-disposed toward the National Park Service. However, if the newspapers and TV say that half the park is burned, and the park also says that half the park is burned, and then the TV and newspapers show you a wall of flame, while the park shows you a single tree burning on a ridge crest 2 ½ miles away, there's a perceptible shift in authority. The truth is somewhere in between, we assume, less dramatic than the TV images, but more to it than the tone the park has taken would lead one to believe. In between is not right on. Right on is what gives authority. Especially with us. We have a sacred right to question authority. When this right is abused, it can lead to anti-intellectualism. The plus side of our famous anti-intellectualism is that we do not easily gainsay the authority of our experience. It *could* be that half the park is burned. That would be the other half. We'll take a look.

With just enough light left to start supper, I camped at Tower Falls campground. It is an awful campground, as are all Yellowstone campgrounds. I rolled my sleeping bag out on a site that was perfectly level because it was a wood frame filled to the gunwales with gravel. The place for my car was also gravelled for drainage. A suburban back yard is closer to nature undisturbed. It is obvious why the campgrounds are so grim: the park has the choice of confining and intensifying the damage or letting it spread. The result is a broad hint that humans are not to feel at home or welcome, as it should be.

While waiting for the water to boil, I obeyed the instruction on a sign at the campground entrance to tune my radio to 1610 for a message:

> Yellowstone National Park is home to both black and grizzly bears. You are a visitor to the home of these and other wild animals. While many of the wildlife may appear tolerant to the presence of people, their behavior is unpredictable and they may charge or attack at any time.... A bear's sense of smell is a thousand times more keen than

a human's and your food or garbage can attract a bear.... It is not advisable to wander around campgrounds in the dark. When this is necessary, make noise, use a flashlight and whenever possible, travel with someone else.... Every visitor to the park has a shared responsibility for the future of the bear. We must all follow these special regulations to avoid bear related property damages, human injuries, and the potential loss of a bear.

A thousand times! The poor guy must be able to smell the pulp mills in Tacoma and Camas.

The sky was so dark gray at sunrise that I assumed that there were clouds above the smoke. However, at 0730, at 8150' on the road to Canyon a red sun, like the insignia on the aluminum fuselage of a kamikaze, floated in the metallic gray sky fifteen degrees above a point I deemed the horizon.

The road from Tower Falls to Canyon runs along a ridge that is at once the west rim of the Grand Canyon of the Yellowstone, and the north ridge of Mount Washburn. Where the paved road traverses from the ridge across the west slope to Dunraven Pass a dirt road continues on up the ridge. I looked up and what should I dimly see but the firetower. What could compare to the summit of Mt. Washburn as the place from which to witness the wildfire of the century?

It seemed that a person who climbs a mountain on fire ought to be carrying water. So I continued on over Dunraven Pass to the picnic area, to find it closed, down to the junction at Canyon to fill a water bottle at the gas station. There was a pickup parked at the junction. A man was lifting a barrier out of the bed. I recalled the flames I'd seen on the ridge to the west at Dunraven Pass. Even though the man was not in uniform, it seemed possible that there might be a connection between those flames and that assemblage of yellow slats he had in his hands. I didn't wait to see what he was going to do next with them, put them in the middle of the road as a barrier, for example. As he turned his attention to a car approaching from the south, I just blithely left the gas station and drove back up toward the pass, preserving deniability by not looking back in the rear view mirror.

Across the pass I found a turnout in an open area along the west slope where there were no trees within several hundred yards in any direction. The dirt road up the ridge was just 75 feet above. Traffic had picked up, and all the vehicles that passed had firefighters in them. I packed a lunch hastily, fearing that someone would stop to inquire about my intentions.

I had just reached the dirt road when a large red carryall came up the road. In it were two young men wearing the yellow shirts and olive drab pants.

"Out for a hike?"

"Yes."

"Going to the top?"

"No, I don't think so; it's pretty smoky."

"It's due to clear up between 10 and 11; we're hoping it will so we can see something too."

"Are those shirts fire-retardant? All the different groups of firefighters seem to be wearing them."

"Yeah, we all look the same. Good old nomex, it doesn't flame. If you get a spark on you it chars nicely all the way through."

They drove up the road 300 yards and stopped to talk to a man and a woman descending the road in a pickup. The people in the pick-up waved to me on their way down the road. I relaxed and had a delightful walk up the mountain until I was turned back by the crew of three forest rangers on the ridge just below the summit.

"Hi there, hahrya doin."

"Fine, breathing a little smoke."

The conversation was interrupted for a moment by the radio, and started over.

"So, hahrya doin?" At this point I knew two things: I was going to be turned back and they weren't used to doing enforcement work. He had been composing what he was going to say as I came up the road. When the radio interrupted him, he started again at the beginning.

"Fine," I said.

"Thing is, this area's closed. We might be starting a backfire here later in the day and it might get a little dangerous around here." And then before I could say anything in reply, "Doggone, you get turned back just when you are almost at the top!" he said with a winning grin. It wouldn't take him long to learn to do enforcement work.

I knew exactly what to do, and began enjoying being on the front side of the badge. I was going to go to the top, one way or another so I did not argue. For appearance sake I remarked that I might have been told a 1000' lower, shrugged my shoulders, turned, and headed down. Any of the excellent points I might have made in favor of my continuing on up from this point so near the summit, if spoken, might elicit from him something more confining than the phrase, "this area." "This area" at this moment meant the ridge we were on. The next ridge to the east was a different area. On the way down I continued past a grove of trees that would have provided cover to the ridge, emerged from the other side in plain view if in case someone was watching, continued on down the road past another place where a gully temporarily blocked their view of me, back into their clear view again, on down finally to where the smoke obscured them nearly completely; and it was but ten steps to the trees. I had given up 800 feet of altitude to insure that they not be disturbed at their work, which I did not believe included lighting a backfire anywhere near their position just below the summit of the mountain. A backfire is started to be sucked into the main fire by the wind created by the rising heat of the fire, preemptively consuming the fuel in advance of the main fire. If the fire got large enough to suck the rising heat of the backfire downhill into it, the mountainside would be burned anyway. He said that they might light a backfire because he wasn't an accomplished liar. I liked him. I didn't want to piss him off. I made a private deal. I wouldn't mind if they didn't tell me their real business if they didn't mind me not telling them mine. We were all in the same business that day, firefighters on duty, firefighters off duty, and me: watching the fire of the century burn because watch was all any of us could do.

Which brings me back to my perch below the summit.

I really wanted to see the fire before I left. My choices were that I could be across the gully and looking down to Dunraven Pass in five to ten steps, or I could turn around right there. Seeing the fire wouldn't change anything down on the pass; and it would be nice not to be seen. To cross the gully unseen, I would have to walk slowly, trying to match

my pace to the motion of the smoke. If I rushed across, a person looking at the white smoke columns would catch the motion out of the
corner of their eye. What the heck, I'd come this far. I avoided looking
up at the tower as I stepped into its view, in case the Elizabethan poets
were right that rays of sight gleamed from, as well as into, eyes.

Across, hunkered down in the rocks, I studied my prospects. The
fire was not at the pass yet but it had covered more than three fourths
of the way it had to go from where it was four hours earlier. The wind
had been rising since I began the traverse around the summit. I could
no longer hear people talking. Time to go.

I stepped off the trail around the summit on to the road . . . into the
roar of a car engine! It was the two guys in the red carryall. They had
been watching what I'd been watching, the fire make its way down
toward Dunraven Pass, had obviously come to my conclusion, and had
driven up to the shoulder where it was wide enough to turn around.
We waved and headed down by our respective routes. I no longer both-
ered to stay out of sight. Since mine was undoubtedly the only civilian
car on the whole 19 mile stretch of road, I assumed that my presence
somewhere on the mountain had been known for hours. I expected to
be having a conversation with a ranger at one end or the other of the
road between Tower Falls and Canyon Village. The problem was to
figure out which end it was to be. I watched, from some six or seven
hundred feet up the ridge, when down on the road the carryall pulled
in behind my car. They were studying the fire. On the slope between us
a doe and buck grazed nonchalantly, they glanced at me and at the fire
but did not seem particularly impressed by either.

Good, the guys in the carryall were going to give the pass a try. If
they didn't come back, then I'd give it a try too. As I waited I considered whether I would have gone back up if it had been a park ranger
instead of a forest service firefighter that had told me that the area
was closed. Probably not, I decided.

The yellow slip on my car was not unexpected, until I read it. It said:
"This is a WARNING—the items checked above were left unsecured. A
$25.00 CITATION will be issued if they are again left unsecured during
the day or night." The items listed were, food, cooking, utensils, bever-
age cans, pet food bowls, ice chests (even if empty); stove, grill and/or

hibachi, dirty dish water and/or water jugs, trash and garbage from fire pit. None of them were checked. Instead there was a note, "All your windows need to be closed tight! Bears have broken into cars this year," and the ranger's signature. I had left my windows cracked for ventilation.

In the pass the flames were well within four hundred yards from the road, maybe within two hundred. I was never very good at judging linear distance up a steep slope. Whole trees flared up, just like on TV. The fire seemed but an image of itself as it would not have had I gotten out of the car to listen to the fire and felt its heat. Someone had posted beside the road a hand lettered sign that read, "No off road travel." No off road travel? Was this a message to me? My car down the road could have inspired the sign, but it seemed addressed to drivers of all-terrain vehicles. There is a story about a Yellowstone ranger who caught a guy with a motorcycle in the backcountry and made him dismantle it and pack it out on pack horses. If the message was meant for me, why was the sign on the pass and not on my car? And in either location it was locking the barn door after the horse was out. The material the ranger at the entrance station gave me said the following:

> Prolonged hot, dry conditions may cause extreme fire danger, Be sure your campfires are completely out before retiring for the night or leaving your campsite. Backcountry campers: campfires may be prohibited in the backcountry. Check with a ranger when you plan your hike. Carefully extinguish all cigarettes and matches, and dispose of them in ashtrays or garbage cans.

I hadn't checked in with a ranger, but the instructions to do so are in the context of a camping trip not a hike up a road as I had been doing when they turned me back. How would the logic go? There are two kinds of travel, on road and off road. Hiking up a ridge is off road travel. So is ballooning. Hitchhiking is on road travel, and skateboarding. I was making a case, a rather pathetic one. Such becomes the discourse when the enforcement authority can no longer rely on the good will of those he would regulate, something I had learned from the other side of the badge two de-cades ago when I was a ranger at Jenny Lake.

In 1966, the Park Service decided to close the climbers' campground at Jenny Lake. I was almost relieved. From a small overflow camp for climber's in 1959, the C-Camp had burgeoned into a dusty, crowded, outdoorsperson's version of Haight-Ashbury. It was a question as to whether hippies-for-the-summer didn't outnumber authentic climb-ers. They certainly outnumbered the "old" climbers of five or more years of experience.

As the number and kinds of people visiting the parks increased, as the Park Service experienced successive cuts in budget because we could not have guns, butter *and* backcountry rangers, and as the Con-gress provided new money only for riot prevention, police work be-came the venue for those wishing to follow the money into positions of power and responsibility within the service. Less like the unarmed British Bobby and more like the highway patrolman became the new model for rangering.

That was a long time ago, in times that were hard on everybody. I was willing to forget it if they were.

I came up alongside of the ranger at the barricade my window down and question ready, "Is that the way to Fishing Bridge, and can I get through to the South Entrance that way?"

"Say, would you pull in right over there across the road? I'd like to talk with you a bit."

His uniform was a kind of a field uniform I hadn't seen before; he was wearing a baseball cap, his skin was appropriately weathered, and he had a red bandanna around his neck. He was about ten years younger than me which still gave him time to have put in the twenty years his gold badge signified—or used to.

"I noticed your car parked up on the road and I wondered what you were doing?" he asked in a friendly tone of polite curiosity, as if it was a nice little chat that he wanted.

"I took a hike up the road up Mount Washburn."

"To the top?" he said as if impressed.

"No, no—just to within maybe 500 feet of the top," I rough esti-mated, rounding off down the next half thousand.

"Oh?" he said, not a doubting oh, a well-I'll-be-darned oh. "Park at Dunraven Pass?"

I gave him a quick puzzled glance, to let him know that I had noticed that he had apparently forgotten that he said he had seen my car: "No, I parked in a turnout that has no trees near it. There seemed to be a fire burning to the west, and I wanted to park where there was no fuel. It's not very far around the corner from where the road starts up," I said patiently.

"Oh," he said (a what-do-you-know-about-that oh) continuing to use Columbo's interview technique. "Did you come in real early this morning?"

"No not real early—oh you mean into the park. I came in last night and camped at Tower Falls Campground," I said. The fact that I was in the campground was verifiable by the fee envelope. He either had to ask me the question he really wanted to know the answer to, and thereby acknowledge that he been acting coy, or drop it. Before he could drop it he had just one more point to establish.

"Did you talk to the ranger?"

"What ranger?"

"Oh," (an how-dense-of-me-it's-all-coming-clear-to-me-now oh), "there was no ranger! You must have missed the ranger. Came in real late?"

"No, I camped just after sunset and left the campground just after sunrise. I started hiking at about 0830."

"Oh," (a well-that-settles-it oh). "Well just for your interest, the backcountry is closed. We saw your car up there and wondered if you were all right."

"When I came over Dunraven Pass, just now, I saw a sign that said, 'No off road travel.' I wondered if that referred just to vehicles or to hiking too."

"No, that includes your feet."

Since he'd said he wanted to talk to me, and we'd about exhausted the topic of my morning's movements, I introduced a new topic.

I showed him my warning: "When I came back, this was on my car."

"You had your windows cracked for ventilation. A bear will hook his claws right over the glass and pull it out. It's happened this year. Especially if they see a cooler," he said nodding toward my cooler, "they know what a cooler is."

"Yes, I suppose they do."

"South Entrance you say, by Fishing Village. Yes you can go that way, right straight down that road."

"Thank you. Sorry if I caused you any worry."

"That's all right. We're happy to see you're safely out of the woods."

I smiled as I drove off, in admiration of his skill. I can't imagine what you'd have to do to make that ranger flap. If I also felt ill at ease, it wasn't because I ignored an order given for my own protection—I'm willing to assume responsibility for my own safety—it was because in order to have been successful as a park ranger, as I once wished to be, I would have had to have become as good as that ranger was at managing people. There was another bothersome thing. At what point does a uniform become a costume? The ranger's garb struck me as costume, designed to deal with people not the elements. Was it that the profession that almost became mine no longer existed, or was it that it never had? Is there any work where you can deal directly with the world as created? Farming? The banker has as much of the farmer's attention than the weather.

I was alone on this trip, but talked to aplenty by signs, persons at information desks, displays, the radio, by protectors of the public lands. The clearest communique had been Wayne's. He had said that his job as a smokejumper was to talk about being the type of smokejumper who puts out fires and talks about putting out fires, for the unambiguous purpose of keeping their budget allocations. I didn't know why budget allocations were a problem for the Aerial Fire Depot, but I believed that whatever the reasons were, they were sufficient to motivate Wayne to become as good as he is at what he does.

There was a new message on AM 1610. Except by airplane, a person can't get to Yellowstone without passing through areas of treeless desert so vast as to be consciousness altering. One may find it exciting and liberating, another may be intimidated, most of us feel some of both. Few visitors feel at home. The radio messages are transmitted for only a few miles, less than five, making the listener a member of a comparatively small audience. There is something cozy about these radio messages. They are about the immediate area the listener is in: a bear message for me when I camped, this one was for folks traveling through burn areas. The man with the comforting voice said that I would see places where the fire had burned close to the road, or even right over the road. I should not be alarmed if I even saw small patches of fire; the roads were constantly patrolled and the situation monitored. There were some words of caution. I should stay in my vehicle, not walk in burned areas because there may be hot spots, drive slowly with headlights on in these smoky conditions, watching for fire crews and equipment, and not stop in the middle of the road.

The story followed the cautionary bits. I was having a unique experience. I should note that the fire burned in a mosaic pattern so that there was considerable green within the burned area. Yellowstone was also having an experience. It was experiencing the driest summer in recorded history—resulting in an unusually large number of fires caused by lightning from thunderstorms. Some fires were being fought aggressively on some fronts.

Their first task was our safety.

Then there was a little segment to the effect that fire is natural and the forest knows it. Fire is one of the most important events in the entire forest ecosystem, it allows sunlight to get to the forest floor, permitting new growth. The lodgepole I saw around me grew after past fires. In a sense I was witness to history being made. Studies show that three or four hundred years ago there were fires like those of this year and we could expect history to repeat itself in the 23d or 24th century.

The radio message was not essentially different in content from printed material about the fire given to me at the gate. The difference was in the sense I got of being told a story. Since the story was about what was outside of the windows of my car, it was not unlike watching a PBS documentary, not the real thing but as close as one can get. I'd been in the car too long.

I hadn't see any charred trees from earlier fires until West Thumb, 70 miles from the North Entrance. From there on down to the South

Entrance, and beyond, there were plenty of burned trees. With the rising wind came plenty of new fire. Just north of the South Entrance I looked across the Lewis River and counted eight brand new smokes in an area the size of a quarter-section. Here was the half of the park that was burned.

The view from Jack Dornan's bar in Moose is, if not the best of any bar in the world, it is one of the serious contenders. I stopped there to sort of fix the view in my mind. Everyone in the West this year will have their own image of the fire. Mine is the view of the Tetons while driving down the inside highway between Moran and Moose. Jackson Hole was my home base for fourteen years; I spent no less than three and a half months of every year in The Valley, looking at those mountains. I can't help looking at the mountains. People whose grandparents were born there can't help it. The view was a dim outline of the Tetons seen through a curtain of dirty gray gauze—not even a silhouette but the shadow of it if a silhouette could cast a shadow. I've never seen anything quite like it: not the darkening of storms or the veil of snow, fog. Both snow and fog carry still within them the special brightness of alpine light. It was as if the fire had not so much obscured as consumed and extracted from the mountain air its light, as cancer takes joy from the face of one we love.

Finding work and home

Jackson, Wyoming would be my home town if I had a home town. I'm the only one in my nuclear family, wife, three kids two grandkids, who wasn't born in Jackson. My parents and grandparents and great-grandparents are from Maine; I'm from Maine though my mother decided to have me in Boston. Sons two and three, Ernest and David, were born in Maine in different towns. We lived in five different towns in Maine during the depression, while my father looked for work, before moving to the Navy Base in Middletown, Rhode Island for the war. Son four, Robert, was born in Rhode Island. The fifth and last child, Kirk, was born in Norfolk, Connecticut, which became home town also to Ernie, Dave, and Bob but not me. I didn't live there long enough. Ernie and Kirk still live there, and Bob and Dave are less than a morning's drive away, but I only went to school there three years, then four years of high school in Torrington, then a couple of years of college, then the army. When I got out of the army, in August 1958, I went directly to Jackson Hole to learn how to climb real mountains. In September, I went back to Hanover, New Hampshire to spend the fall and my army savings on college. I returned to Jackson in December, to become a skiing and climbing bum, later a mountain rescue ranger; then I was that in the summer and a student at the University of Wyoming in the winter, and then student at the University of Washington in the winters; then I became a mountain guide in the summers and professor at Wyoming in the winters—until, in 1971, I became only a professor at The Evergreen State College in Olympia, Washington and not a mountaineer or from Jackson's Hole, Wyoming anymore.

I have lived in Olympia longer than at least half the people now there, but Olympia is not my hometown, nor is any place else. Everybody in America is from somewhere else, including most Native Americans, who are all spiritually and many physically displaced from where they were at the time of contact. There must also be many people who, like me, aren't from some other particular place, uprooted, as we were, by the depression and the war, or by economic expansion, or urbanization, or the various "flights to" or from. We do not feel like orphans or refugees. We *are* more or less constantly involved in a search for our place, but this search for place seems to us like the exercise of an American privilege, an actual right guaranteed by our story if not our Constitution. I have stopped, or rather slowed, my search for my place. I feel at home any place north of San Francisco and west of Devil's Tower—which means, I fully acknowledge, that I have not connected myself to a place but to the romantic landscape of the West. I've gotten old enough to stop being ashamed of being accused of being a romantic. Most of the realists I know are just romantics slightly deficient in imagination.

My main business in Jackson was to become a grandfather. Melanie, my oldest daughter, was due to have a baby on September 16. I was there to cover the first half of the month; Connie, grandmother-to-be and a nurse, was coming later because she was betting the baby would be late. I called Melanie from Lewiston, Missoula, and Yellowstone, keeping her informed of my halting progress. Melanie was happy to see me finally arrive: partly because Carol, her cousin and breathing coach, was going to be gone for a couple of days, mainly because she needed my car. My son Kirk, who had come a week earlier, was up in the mountains, hiking with Larry, a neighbor of ours. We needed to leave a car for them at the trail head.

On television news the night I arrived in Jackson, the Yellowstone Fire was spelling relief from the election coverage. Discourse about the let burn policy in parks and wilderness areas of the Forest Service, which had gone on in Jackson for years, had recently gotten hot.

Against a backdrop of flames, television provided a platform for experts—biologists, park superintendents, spokespersons for the Sierra Club and spokespersons for the Wyoming Outfitters—to present their views to the public for their consideration. Television news does this in a disinterested manner. The reporter isn't supposed to have a view, but is allowed to be sympathetic. In their role as disengaged avuncular sympathizers, they cast the firefighters both as heroes and quasi-victims. Not unlike the television roles of troops during the Viet Nam War. There were in fact so many overt and implied images of combat in the coverage that one might think that the military was called in to make the war analogy literal. The non-combatants make their appearance as hero/victims too. There was that night an interview of a woman whose business wasn't doing well because there were fewer tourists. She and her husband "sold everything" and came west (we know our lines, there should be special U-Hauls with Conestoga shaped tops). Now they might lose it all. In my town, four small businesses in a three-block area failed that year without even making the local paper. If you are already west, you are not entitled to the sympathy afforded persons who have come west seeking a new life and not finding it. (The convention is that the hardships of going west are supposed to be more threatened than actual—not unlike the wilderness experience in National Parks.) These reminders of known stories, Vietnam and the western frontier, provide a context—familiarity and weight, we might say—to the story of the fires. The dramatic tension turned on whether or not the administrators of the let burn policy would be exposed as the authors of the disaster, their thinking unduly influenced by environmental extremists.

The issue became, as it often does when the discourse is managed by journalists, one of credibility, the credibility of park officials as managers. Interestingly, there were few challenges to the assertion that there has to be fire in the park's ecological mix. What was asserted was that the fire has to be managed. The "disaster" was the result of the incredible, in the view of the accusers, practice of allowing lightning to select where the fires should be, and weather determining their size and duration, instead of a program of prescribed burning. Even more incredible to the critics was the practice of not fighting the fire with every conceivable technological weapon available.

Ever since I started up over Lolo Pass four days earlier, I'd been referencing the past and thinking about the mutability of things and lives, normal enough, after a long absence from people and places, but intensified by the fire. The smoke drifting around in the landscape seemed a stage prop for dimming memory. There were no sharp scenes taking me right back; all that was familiar was strangely familiar. On television, a woman being interviewed made a remark I heard again that day and was to hear many times in the three weeks I was in the area, "I'm sad that my children's children will never see the Yellowstone we knew."

It was while watching television that evening that I became concerned about how the Park Service was doing. That same woman prefaced her remark with, "I know we are supposed to look at it as historic, but..." She was quoting the park's radio message to television. Tom Brokaw said at the close of that same segment of the broadcast, "In fairness we should point out what the park people like to point out—that there are nearly 9000 people fighting the fires within the park without losing a building or a facility or there being a serious injury."

I groaned to my daughter, "I can't believe they set themselves up like that. They just made the credibility of their entire management procedure depend on whether they lose a building or somebody gets killed."

The southwest wind continued through the night, clearing the

smoke out of the valley by morning. The next morning, an old climbing friend from the early sixties, Irene Beardsley, called. I had been
thinking of Irene. Connie and Irene had been hiking together the
morning that Connie went into labor with our youngest daughter,
Summer. We'd been out of touch with Irene for several years. Then
she and her new-to-us husband, Dan, stopped by to see us the previous summer, and so we were in touch again. Irene and Dan were
near the end of a two-week hiking and climbing stay in the valley.
She called to invite me to have dinner that evening with them and
Bob Irvine, my replacement at the Jenny Lake Ranger Station. She
also mentioned that she had hoped to get Dan up the Grand, but was
reluctant, "in my present advanced state of decrepitude," to go up
with just the two of them because she wasn't sure she could hold the
weight of a fall. Also, it almost appeared they'd have to do it in one
day now unless they wanted to climb the Grand Teton, come down,
and drive straight through to Palo Alto. I hadn't been asked, but I
said, "Not me!" just in case. Ten minutes later, I called Irene back.
"Why don't we climb the Grand Friday, in one day?" After an almost
imperceptible pause, I assume for Irene to silently view the prospect
of having to haul both Dan and me up the mountain, we agreed.

I had quit climbing pretty cleanly seventeen years before when I
stopped guiding and left Wyoming. I quit mainly because I wouldn't
be able to stay in climbing shape, which requires psychological as
well as physical conditioning. I had long had a private pact with the
mountains not to show them contempt by going into them unready.
To my credit, I did not believe that this practice would keep me from
getting killed in the mountains, just keep me from being killed for
being stupid. I also quit because I thought I ought to stop cashing in
on the wilderness. It took me years to get my thoughts about it straight.

It was clear by 1971 that tens of thousands of environmentally
conscious people in the wilderness would only take a little longer to
destroy it than tens of thousands of environmental slobs. By 1971
professional mountaineers began to fathom our complicity in the destruction of the wilderness. Teaching people to climb insured that
humans gained access to every last bit of wilderness, with fewer of
them getting killed on the way, encouraging more to follow. The guid-

ing profession began in Europe with English gentlemen hiring resi-
dents of Alpine villages to accompany them up the mountains. The
clients were at first as technically good at climbing as the guides.
That history is repeating itself in the Himalayas in our time more
systematically with climbing schools having been set up to teach
Sherpas technical climbing. American guides love to guide highly
skilled climbers, but to make a minimum living as a guide, you have
to teach a sizable bunch of novices per summer how to climb.

I didn't think that my friends who were guides should do as I did.
These guides were professional in a way few guides had been in the
past, when guiding was something you did in the interim between
leaving home and settling down. The majority of Exum Guides in
1971 were within a year or two of having been at it for ten years,
weren't planning on doing anything else, and I didn't think they should
be planning to do anything else. On the other hand, if I shouldn't be
introducing new people to the wilderness, why wasn't that true of
anybody? To say, "Well, I don't know about you, but this is what's
right for me," amounts to a disclaimer that the issue is an ethical one.
It becomes something like a matter of taste. Sometimes the ethical
equation simply cannot be resolved.

I finally decided that I gave up being a professional mountaineer
because I didn't have to do it, and contributing to the destruction of
the wilderness is something you should do only if you have to. I think
a logger and I might agree about that much. My way of knowing that
I didn't have to be a mountaineer was that I no longer wanted to get
better at climbing. To continue mountain guiding after no longer wanting to get better at it would be, I decided, like continuing to teach
having lost interest in learning. I don't know why some climbers have
to teach others to climb and some don't. It was obvious that my late
colleague, Willi Unsoeld just *had* to teach people to climb, but not
obvious why. I did persuade him that taking students to sea would be
better than taking them into the mountains because the sea was harder
to damage. He was scheduled to teach in a marine studies program
the fall after he died. He died leading a group of students out of a
storm on Mt. Rainier (not a bad exit). I reserved to myself the privilege of climbing again should I feel ready, or should the damage to

the mountains become as bad as it was going to get. In the ten minutes it took me to call Irene back, I realized that I was very much ready to climb the Grand with her once more. In the seventeen years since I left, the water in the high meadows has become polluted and they have installed a solar powered shithouse at the Lower Saddle—emptied periodically by helicopter. That's certainly bad enough to allow me back on the mountain.

Twenty years ago, Irene, her family, and Irene's former husband, Leigh, built a small place on a chunk of sagebrush flats south of the airport. The land had little value in itself, though with serious irrigation it will produce grass, but the entire Teton Range is draped above their west property line: to the north are hung the Absarokas; the Gros Ventre Range murals the eastern horizon. From the back yard, where I parked my car, I could see the ski areas above Jackson and Teton Village. They've acquired neighbors, making the land of slightly less personal value to them, but since the Rockerfellers and the Schenleys are discrete and considerate, and certainly have not diminished the value of the land, there is little to complain of. Dan was over to the neighbors' talking irrigation, still done by the old fashioned method of moving canvas dams around in the ditches to cause them to overflow in the desired places. The dams themselves were of new-fashioned orange plastic.

In a few minutes Bob Irvine arrived. There have been four rangers-in-charge at Jenny Lake since the founding of the rescue team. Dick Emerson, was a seasonal ranger for eleven years, at Jenny Lake for eight years. Tim Bond replaced Dick in the summer of 1960. Tim died in a climbing accident eight weeks later and I replaced him. Bob replaced me eight years later and has been there, now, longer than the rest of us put together. The number of citations and Department of Interior Valor Awards accruing to the team, or individuals in his teams, have *more* than doubled in his tenure. It is a remarkable record. I admire his staying in physical and psychological condition to do the climbing. More than that, I am amazed that Irvine, who when he worked for me was as principled a person as any I knew, and as stiff-necked about them, survived the succession of "permanent" people who nominally outranked him: Assistant District Rangers, District

Rangers, Chief Rangers, and Superintendents. It is very tempting for an ambitious, but slightly insecure, career ranger who's legitimate authority in knowledge of the park, the district, climbing, or rescuing is far less than Bob's, to try to gain some authority by a show of power. It certainly helps to always be in the right, which I found impossible and Bob seemed to find effortless, but sometimes that's not enough. I had heard rumors of a time when it appeared Bob might have to leave, but he never told me the story of that. Irvine has been known to grumble, but a whiner he is not.

Bob Irvine showed up wearing his "A Woman's Place is on Top" tee shirt. Since Irene got on top of Annapurna in 1979, Irvine has preserved that tee shirt through a decade. To tease him, and to reassure ourselves that neither of us had changed that much, I told Bob about my two hikes up Mt. Washburn and conversation with the ranger. His response was entirely satisfactory: "We call that willful misunderstanding," he said crisply. The conversation went back and forth between old times, the intervening gap, and the present, mainly the fire.

During dinner, I mentioned that I was concerned about a public relations disaster for the park, and there ensued another of the discussions of whether or not, once you decide to fight the fire, you use every technological weapon at your disposal. Irvine was in favor of chainsaws but against bulldozers. His reasoning was that the park had to respond politically—as the only action that might accomplish anything, nobody was going to do anything effective about the fires— and what the concessionaires wanted would have more influence on future fire management policy than the scientists.

I asked Bob what he thought motivated the people who opposed natural regulation. Two things he thought: they can't stand the suggestion that humans might not be in charge, and they are horrified at the sight of a burning tree. Why horrified? Because forty years of Smokey the Bear have brainwashed them into believing that a forest fire is evil. They think it's a waste. If they can't use it for studs or pulp, and the tree's not going to stand there coloring the landscape green, then it's a waste. Since the tourists never go into the forest, they don't know that nothing grows underneath the canopy of a stand of lodgepole pine. Until it burns the forest can't renew itself.

Irene suggested that the maintenance people just spray the road-sides with green paint. It's cheaper than making a show of trying to put out the fires. Bob told us that, when this same topic was discussed at Dunbar Susong's retirement party a few days earlier, Dunbar's view had been that they should have fought all the fires early with all means possible, because of the political consequences of the now enormous cost of fighting the fire. This surprised me; I didn't understand it; but I took it seriously. Dunbar did not compromise principle in general and in particular not for political reasons. Dunbar was my immediate supervisor at the time I stopped working at Jenny Lake, and with me, loser of many political battles. He left Grand Teton to spend the remainder of his career in the most remote ranger station in Yellowstone, barricaded against promotions that would have put him permanently behind a desk.

Talk of the fire consumed most of the evening, but we managed a few other bits of conversation. For Dan's benefit, we began to talk about rangering then and now, after one thought of the future. It was about helicopters. Helicopters are addicting. It's impossible not to use one if one is available. The price for the convenience of helicopters is the possibility that a small mechanical failure or pilot error will wipe out the rescue team. We agreed that all you can do about that is not think about it.

We thought instead of old times when we were brand new rangers. One of the photographs most prized by visitors is that of a bull moose belly deep in a pond, head up, and water cascading off his rack. Bob told about the time a visitor asked our colleague, Rick Reese, when he was a brand new ranger, what moose ate when they had their heads under the water. Rick, decked out in green suit, badge, and flat-brimmed hat, could not bring himself to say that he didn't know.

"He thought, 'I'm a ranger; I'm supposed to know this stuff.' He asked himself what had he seen at the bottom of these ponds and remembered salamanders. So that's what he said, 'Salamanders.'" Rick went on to become an important environmentalist and nature educator, but, whatever the rest of the world thinks of you, only your homeboys know, and have forgiven, all.

Other topics of conversation were the impending marriage of Renny Jackson, the most decorated rescue ranger in the park service, and Alex Lowe, the young climber who recently did the grand traverse in nine and a half hours. The grand traverse is the summits of Teewinot, Owen, the Grand, the Middle, South Teton, and all the little summits between the South Teton and the summit of Nez Perce, beginning and finishing at the Lupine Meadows Trailhead. When I worked here, people were still imagining a time when that traverse might be done in less than a day. "The standards of climbing are now such," said Bob, "that a serious climber can't climb himself into shape. He or she has to be on a year round gymnastic training schedule."

With that I went back to town, the next day to get ready to do what used to pass as making a climb.

There have been changes in foot gear. They make really skinny rock climbing shoes, with soles, I am told, made out of material that molds itself to the rock and hangs on by itself. They also have lighter weight mountaineering, "boots" that are sneakers ("plimsoles" if you're a Brit) with cleated soles. With these developments in mind, I called Tom Kimbrough at the Jenny Lake Ranger Station.

"Tom, I understand that a person is not allowed to go into the mountains without the latest in lightweight footgear?"

"That's right; we won't even sign you out if you're not wearing your multi-colored lycra tights."

In fact Tom hikes in wearing an old pair of leather boots and then switches to higher technology. I called hoping to hear that there were folks who still used the old gear, but was a little disappointed not to be advised to buy the latest thing. What I really wanted from Tom was permission to buy expensive shoes that I might use only this once. The season was about over. Stuff was on sale in the sporting goods stores. Even so, rock shoes were a hundred bucks. I'd be shedding weight at about five dollars per ounce. Owning these shoes, designed for people who climb on holds not clearly visible to the naked eye, would make me be about as technologically appropriate as using a laser beam to light my wood stove. Instead of the rock shoes, I bought the sneakers with cleated soles; they would be at least as good on the rock as the first boots I ever owned, and were so light as to seem like outright cheating on the trail.

Irene, Dan and I went up to the ranger station at Jenny Lake to sign out for the climb at the same time as the evacuees from Old Faithful were coming south. Tom Kimbrough and Leo Larson were on duty, Leo helping a couple who were signing out for a backcountry trip, Tom reading Stephan Hawkin's book. Tom was just starting to explain the universe to me when a woman opened the door, stepped in, asked directions to Jackson in a vaguely Eastern urban accent, and, before directions could be given, interrupting herself almost, said, "We've just come down from Old Faithful; we had reservations at the Inn for two more days."

"Well," said Kimbrough in his richly timbred Tennessee voice, as he drew a high stool up to the counter, sat on it, gripped one knee with both hands, and settled slowly back—sweeping the rest of us into her audience with a rotation of his eyes before locking onto hers—"let us hear all about it."

As she did, leaning forward on the counter into the embrace of Tom's attention, Tom prompting her, I thought how fortunate she was to have Tom as the first person to tell her story to. Leo noticed me smiling and, nodding his head in agreement, murmured to me, "He's good." What Tom is good at is using his weathered skin, big smile, some gray in the hair, and calm, slow speech to convey to the visitor, "Well yes, as a matter of fact, it *can* get pretty western around here, but, as you see, we're doing fine and you will too. Of course we have to warn you about the bears and suchlike, lawsuits you know, and you also know that some folks have no sense at all—no matter where they're from; but you should be here to relax and enjoy nature's magic; we're here to let you know if it looks like she is going to get out of hand." No need for me to come back to the ranger station, everything was in excellent hands.

Holding on

The next day we climbed the Grand. Where the road north out of Jackson climbs up out of the Flat Creek drainage in the Elk Refuge, and reaches the end of East Gros Ventre Butte, is where the view of the Tetons lines the western horizon.

Hard to maintain a preoccupation there. As often as not it's a moment for a change of thought. My thought had been that it was about 0430 and I'd gone to bed at 1230. My new thought, apropos of nothing immediate, was that because of our "two or three-minded relationship with the land we live in a corresponding ethical condition." Leave it to a Yankee to make a little outing for old times sake problematic. I suppose that the low glow of the fire on the east side of the valley, and the discussions about whether it belonged there or not, brought this thought to mind.

In the car from Irene & Dan's to the Lupine Meadow parking lot, "We're allowed this aren't we Irene?" The referent of "this" was the fact that we were borrowing ropes from the rescue cache, thanks to Kimbrough (we'd probed Irvine gently at dinner about this possibility but found good solid Irvine), and had access to the hut on the Saddle, and my new lightweight shoes. "We've earned this because of our great contributions in the past to American mountaineering, right?" Irene didn't reply—because she was perhaps thinking that we were allowed this because we are in a "too advanced state of decrepitude" to get up the mountain any other way.

It was the beginning of a day of nagging little problems of body and spirit. We'd both forgotten many important specifics about the Exum Route: bad news about the state of our memory, good news about our route-finding ability. We were never more than 50 feet off route and didn't have to backtrack anywhere. The best news for me was that though I could not remember the route, I did remember the interesting moves. My body retained the memory of how to maneuver in places I've expected to fall off of since I first climbed it thirty years before. Making the move off of Wall Street felt like the first time I did it. I also remembered how to guide as I got Dan across it.

He wanted to go across lower and I wouldn't let him. Irene later reminded me that it was in fact easier to make the move lower down. "Yes," I said, "but it's not the pure way. He's done it now the pure and never needs to apologize for how he did it." Irene accepted that but did observe further that if we really wanted to do it purely, we'd do as Exum did, jump across.

A little later, I dropped my pack for the first time in my life. Dan recovered it for me.

My next trick was to run out of air two or three hundred feet below the summit. We spent on the summit only sufficient time to take and have taken three photographs: me and Irene, Irene and Dan, the three of us. I thought that this might well be the last time either Irene or I climbed the Grand and that we should perhaps sign the summit register. The other people on the top weren't signing. The register was a mess. Irene, now our tactical leader, wanted to get us, me in particular, off the summit fast, so I jammed the mess of paper back into its plastic tube, cover lost, and headed down.

"Should we sign the register?" asked someone in the other party. "No," replied the biggest guy, "I know what I was doing up here, I don't care if anybody else knows." I thought, "So that's the ethic now," and felt virtuous and lucky that I had escaped making a "quaint" historical notation. I wished I could borrow his confident sense of knowing what he was doing. Why is it that every time I climbed a mountain it was an identity crisis!

There was this exchange at the end of the traverse to the Upper Saddle: "It's amazing how the altitude can knock it out of you. I could hardly stand up on the last three or four hundred feet."

Beyond Dan and Irene, to whom this had been directed, I saw Rod Newcomb, whom I may not have seen for eighteen years, probably then too somewhere on the Exum or Owen-Spalding route. He glanced at me and turned back to his client.

Irene: "Feeling better now?"

Me: "Yes. It went away as quickly as it came. I feel fine now."

Rod: "M'God it's Sinclair! I thought I'd heard that voice before. (Then, after bringing his client up to him.) The only way for people of your age (he's two years older than me) to do this is to do it once a week. (Then he looked at Irene) Ortenburger!"

Irene: "As it was."

Rod: "Huh?"

Irene: (louder and clearer) "As it was! It's Beardsley."

She introduced Dan. I asked Rod why he was climbing the Grand twelve hours later in the day than they usually did. Was it because of the weather?

"Well I've seen it like this before. It's not doing much now (we had been seeing rain falling intermittently on the Idaho side for the past hour) but if it comes up here this time of year it will be snow."

His reply was a little odd: he knew we knew all that. He seemed to be speaking for the benefit of his client, almost avuncular, and politely left it to us to answer our question.

Further down we ran into a larger party led by Pratt and Ken. I asked them the same question and got as a response another question, about the rappell. These old guides were getting hard of hearing. We stopped at the Lower Saddle to return the ropes and the pair of gloves we borrowed from the ranger's rescue cache and to eat the sardines I had brought as emergency food. The emergency was that we wanted the energy in the oil.

The new trail to the Meadow from the Petzoldt Caves seemed interminable going down. It seemed a breeze going up. I told Dan about Willi playing his harmonica for his clients on this stretch. There is a route through the boulders at the exit from the Meadows to the maintained trail. I allow myself to relax only after I get through this place. Irene and I talked about this defense we have against getting careless on the descent. Her fearsome point is the little friction traverse 2/3 of the way down from the Upper to the Lower Saddle. Hers makes more sense—it *is* delicate. I believe some of the guides belay their clients across this. When we crossed this place, after watching Irene cross, I remarked, "Boy, this pitch *has* your attention hasn't it."

"I really don't like this place," was her response. Then I remembered hauling somebody, an Exum client, out of there. I'd not choose for my last feared spot one as hard as is Irene's.

It was quite dark by the time we got to the trail. The weather was still being held on the Idaho Side, damned up by the range, so there were stars, but no moon, and smoke. As usual, I held off using a light for as long as I could. "If you use a light you only see what's in the spot of light. The rest of the mountain, bears, and moose are invisible," I guide-like averred. Irene agreed, but eventually we had to give in to Dan. We had made him go ahead so his light wouldn't ruin our night vision, but in spite of some light from a burning ridge in the Huck Fire, we went down slower and slower until I relented about using the headlamp. Then I couldn't make it work. Dan was in the lead with his flashlight, Irene next, me stumbling along third in the dark. Dan said: "Rock to the right. Rock to the left. Tree root. Water bar. Rock in the center." without cease from the third switchback to the paved trail.

We could have gotten down without the light if we'd been willing to devote the rest of the night to the project, but I worried about people waiting for us. I wished we could have done at least this last easy, safe, section without technological help.

We returned the key to the rescue cache hut to Kimbrough and he made lemonade for us. "You were climbing illegally, you know," he said with a smile.

"Huh?"

"Your climb was illegal after three. The backcountry was closed at three this afternoon."

"The guides must have left from the Lower Saddle at almost exactly that time."

Was there radio contact between the Guide Shack and the Lower Saddle? I wouldn't ask. Maybe someday there'd be a perfect moment to make them nervous about why they were so lucky in getting their clients up before the closure. Did they think of me as still a ranger? That would be all right.

Kimbrough told me I ought and to go to Renny Jackson's wedding reception and to the Jackson Hole Mountain Guides' celebration of the 20th anniversary of its founding, billed as "The End of Mountaineering in the Tetons as We Have Known It."

The Political Fire

The fire was now the lead item daily on television news. There is justness in the feeling of information officers at Yellowstone that the disaster everybody was talking about was not environmental but economic—and that the economic threat to tradesmen and outfitters in the Yellowstone area was trivial compared to the threat to another segment of the entertainment industry, television news. The disaster was not that it was a dry year but that it was an election year. By midsummer, coverage of the presidential election threatened to move beyond boredom into hitherto untouched regions of outright mental anguish and civic embarrassment. The television news industry, stuck with a story it had to cover, felt itself in danger of creating a prolonged period of free aversion therapy for television addicts. Television took the story where television needed it to go to confect the entertainment, and print perforce followed.

Having discovered where the cameras were, members of the cabinet and the candidates showed up, and by then it seemed that the Yellowstone fire season of 1988 may well become the watershed event in the nation's discourse about wilderness. The let burn policy— in effect, President Reagan was shocked to learn, for 16 years— polarized the discourse and the middle ground dramatically shifted so that George Bush became an environmentalist, those who used to be environmentalists became "environmental extremists," and Michael Dukakis was left with nothing to say. Park officials suddenly were transformed from protectors of the wilderness to the perpetrators of an "environmental disaster."

Secretary Hodel, visiting the fires on 10 September, was widely quoted as saying, "I think its devastating. As we've said before, it's a disaster." However, even if it hadn't been called one by a member of the cabinet, the fire would have inevitably been seen as a disaster. We have become so accustomed to the genre, disasters-as-entertainment, on television, that when John Varley, Yellowstone chief of research, told a newspaper reporter that, "There's no ecological bad news here.

In fact, it's very exciting. This is the ecological event of the century,"
he didn't have a chance. Don Despain made the front page of the
Sunday Denver Post with "Burn, baby, burn." That was the headline.
In the text we find it in context. He's watching a plot that they've
marked. "Burn, baby, burn. In 1981 we had a good year. We burned
20,000 acres." The park service guys weren't even trying to be politic. They had no recourse but honesty. I was proud of them, but worried about their future. The Secretary hung them out to dry and all
they could do is to stick to their professional view, presented two
years earlier in 1986 in *Wildlife in Transition*:

> Most researchers, whether they work for a chemical
> company, a state fish and game agency, or a federal ser-
> vice, have some philosophical attachment to at least some
> of their employer's goals. But the responsible researcher
> dare not let those attachments (or the employer's demands)
> get in the way of objective research. Scientific research
> and management policies are different things. Park Ser-
> vice research projects are not aimed at simply supporting
> some established policy. Park Service researchers are not
> obligated to somehow prove that some management di-
> rection is the right one. That's not science; it's public rela-
> tions. What Park Service research is in fact aimed at is
> testing and thereby helping to refine policy. . . . What is
> going on is called "experimental management." It is, in
> the simplest of terms, management that is conducted as a
> scientific experiment so that the results can be evaluated. .
> . . The "great experiment," as it is sometimes called, is a
> test of just to what extent we can let the giant and com-
> plex ecological setting of the northern range take care of
> itself without human involvement. The Park Service is un-
> der no obligation of policy to let the setting alone; if the
> test shows that managers need to take a more active part
> in maintaining some part of the system (for example, by
> controlled burning of vegetation, or controlling the num-
> bers of animals), managers are free to do so.

This kind of discourse, okay for PBS, does not play well on network television news. The park people knew that they weren't playing well. Lacking a forum for a technical discussion, and not so dumb as to attack the media, in an attempt to use the medium itself, they were reduced to asserting that no, then few, then not too many buildings were lost and none of the nearly nine thousand firefighters (40,000 individuals cumulative total for the summer) were killed fighting fires. The Yellowstone Fire was in fact one of the safest places for a person to be this summer, any person, not just a firefighter. Keeping that quantity of people off the highways must have saved half a dozen lives. The park people also knew they weren't playing well because they knew they didn't know enough, and never would, to offer the kind of assurances and predictions that they were being asked for. How much does nature want? When will she stop? The very asking presumes that the rangers, not nature, should be in charge. Although I had in the past disagreements with one thing or another that the Park Service had done, this attack on the authority of the Park Service was not good news for proponents of wilderness. Perceived as infiltrated by environmental terrorists, or as self-serving bureaucrats, their professional disinterestedness was vitiated. The park service has long experience in mediating conflicting interests. You want to keep that.

The park service will not successfully defend natural regulation in the context of a perceived disaster, and will be forced to "manage" fires by prescription burning. We would manage the weather if we could, and have tried. Undoubtedly we would try to stop earthquakes and volcanic eruptions if we could, piping in cold from outer space to freeze tectonic plates and to cool the Earth's core so the plates would stay welded in place. There is no limit to our ambition to rule nature. We can't control weather or tectonic plates, but we can control our forests, by clearcutting them and allowing only our pet trees to grow, for example. Prescription burning, once it becomes policy, would complete the domestication of practically all life on earth.

"Except pestilence," as a Larry pointed out as we discussed this while watching *Platoon* on television, "They'll never domesticate pestilence." Larry is a pediatrician with a shared practice at Group Health, shared in order to give him time to hunt, fish, farm, and travel. He is always roaming over or working on the land. "I love it when Nature shows them who's boss," said Larry. *Platoon* got us to thinking about the outrage people felt during the Viet Nam War at the notion that there were limits to what we could do with our technology, and the fact that there are still people who think we could have had it our way had we really let loose. One of the local papers reported that a fire boss from California was outraged that he had been prevented from using bulldozers in a wilderness area. Even a fire boss from California doesn't believe that he can make a frontal assault on a fire that is spotting (shooting out burning projectiles ahead of itself) a mile and a half. It's the principle he was concerned about. We got bulldozers, let's use them. We may not be able to win against nature but by God we can show her a thing or two. Of course a fire boss from California doesn't think about nature, or what's best for the land, he thinks about doing your best fighting fires. Without the Park Service, a public, professionally disinterested research and public service institution, as credible proponents of the theory and practice of natural regulation, we are left with those who want to cash in on the wilderness versus the "environmental extremists."

"The Greater Yellowstone Coalition" and "The Greater Yellowstone Ecosystem" were terms much in the news, and their founder and author respectively was none other than Rick Reese of salamander-eating-moose fame. Since the baby was not in any hurry to join us here in the world, I went to Salt Lake City to talk to the extremist himself.

Ted and Kathy Wilson decided to take an evening off from running Ted for Governor of Utah on the Democratic ticket to chat with the old man.

Discounting the fact that Rick's body was as hard and lean as a hickory axe handle, I could not help but notice that Rick's hair and beard were definitely grayer than mine, even allowing for the disadvantage he has in having more hair to be gray. Mary Lee looks unchanged except for some smile creases. It was sort of uncanny. Our son, Kirk, developed such a crush on Mary Lee when he was eight years old that he, to this day, keeps falling in love with women exactly the age she was then. It's as if his infatuation has taken her out of time. When Ted and Kathy arrived it seemed that they had changed even less than the rest of us. In Ted's case, I figured he just looked youthful in comparison to all the other politicians on television lately, but I don't know what accounts for Kathy's immortality. In truth, it's not immortality but gracious mortality. Women are never more attractive than they are at the age when in their faces you see at once their youthful beauty and the knowledge and wisdom they have since acquired, more firmness and strength of character in their expressions, more softness in their eyes.

We spent some time reminiscing.

Late June 1970. Ted and I are standing on a just-built, still tentless tent platform on the lower slopes of Rendezvous Peak, the hill on which the new Jackson Hole Ski Area has been constructed. We, Ted, Ray Jacquot, Jack Turner, and I, have just constructed the tent platform. It was to be Ted and Kathy and Benji and Jenny's home for the summer. We built it fairly close to a source of water; we had forgotten about mosquitoes. About an hour earlier, two year old Jenny had fallen off the platform and scraped her forehead. At the moment Ted and I are standing on the platform, Kathy, Benji, and Jenny have just turned south on the Moose-Wilson Road headed for Salt Lake City where they will sleep in beds in a house that night. My own family wasn't in Jackson that summer either. They were in the log house we rented at the base of the Snowy Range 30 miles outside of Laramie.

That scene on the lower slope of Rendezvous Peak did not precisely mark the end of our days as professional mountaineers, but that day was in sight.

I told Ted that three days earlier I had attended the 20th anniversary of the founding of the Jackson Hole Mountain Guides. Out of sixty or more people there, only Tom Kimbrough, Leigh Ortenburger, and Lou Breitenbach remembered me. Those who had heard of me were surprised, and somewhat disappointed, to learn that it wasn't he but me who had opened the guide service. "That's all right," I said, "if I had been them, I would have wanted to think that too. It makes a better story." At this time, Ted was way ahead in the polls but down a little from the 32 percentage points he had earlier. (However, before Ted arrived, Rick reminded me that Utah was 70 percent

Republican and when these Mormons get in the voting booth, they find it almost impossible to make their hands do what they have to do to vote Democratic. Right now they are mad at the incumbent, Rick thought, but no lead was safe for a Democrat in Utah. He thought the race was very close. In the event, Ted lost by a percentage point and a half.)

As with every gathering the talk turned to the fire, swinging on a hinge I provided by mentioning that Leigh Ortenburger had told me that in 1878 W.H. Jackson, the photographer, had left the valley because of smoke; in '79 it was Thomas Moran: Baillie-Gohrman in '80. We deferred to Rick, who had devoted his life full time to wilderness preservation for more than a decade.

"I consider a climax lodgepole pine forest as essentially dead," said Rick about the fire itself. "As you know, nothing grows under the canopy of such a forest. Nature doesn't approve of static situations, and takes steps to change them."

Most of our talk was about people. "People are irrationally frightened of wolves, grizzly, and fire."

Using Irvine's very words: "They believe that we are supposed to be in charge around here and wolves, bears, and fire makes them feel as if they aren't in charge."

It was surprised to hear Rick, this most extreme environmentalist, say (in response to a question about what the park should have done): "Knowing what I know now, in my uncannily perceptive hindsight, I probably would have done more prescribed burning. Some fires actually destroy the soil, bake it right down to mineral soil; probably this one will in some places." In response to my surprise that the fire should have forced him off a position of natural regulation, he pointed out that nobody he knew of, scientist, manager, or environmental politician, ever imagined that natural regulation could be anything more than a matter of degree. "Dunbar has an interesting position," said Rick, " 'What a waste of money to fight these fires this way!' he said, talking about not using chainsaws and motorized vehicles. 'We should have jumped on every one of them using everything we had from the beginning.' He was worried about the political damage to the park service."

I didn't see Dunbar's point at the time, I thought it was a similar to what I understood Irvine's to be: if you fight, fight, if not, not. Upon reflection, I've realized that certainly Dunbar's thought and probably Irvine's too, is more complex than that form of purest view. Their view is that what the public has to be taught is that fire like this can't be managed. Getting that point across would, down the road, save much more country than would be destroyed by bulldozers in the Yellowstone meadows and chainsaws amongst the lodgepoles.

We halted the fire discussion to speak of Dunbar. "Irvine was at his very best. You don't think of Irvine as an orator, but there are times when he can rise to the occasion and say what has to be said better than anybody else could. His theme was that in being there to honor Dunbar's retirement we were in fact 'honoring the retirement of the last remaining field ranger.' When he said that, everybody knew he was right. The Superintendent, Bob Barbee, got up there and muttered something about there being a few other field rangers somewhere, but we knew he was lying. There aren't any others, and there won't be."

Dunbar missed the North Face rescue of 1967 because he was fighting fires in Yellowstone, and was injured. He was a superior example of the service's fiercely loyal critics. The park wanted people managers, of the public, of each other. That is what they rewarded with promotions and praise. To manage people, your own or the public, you have to sit at a desk thinking about policies and money, writing down or talking words and numbers. This activity is pretty much the same whether the building you do it in is in a forest, in a desert, on a seacoast, or in Washington, D.C. You are a park ranger who does little ranging, that's mainly done by seasonals, and the particularity of the place you're in, the particular portion of earth itself for which you are responsible, doesn't much matter with respect to your working life. The park service, naturally, encouraged mobility and discouraged what they disparagingly called, "homesteading," by not promoting you unless you transferred. Dunbar went from assistant district ranger of the south district at Teton, to Yellowstone where he eventually got promoted to, and retired from two decades after leaving Teton, the position of district ranger at Bechler Ranger Station in the southwest corner of Yellowstone, which, because you have to go into Idaho via Livingston, Montana, West Yellowstone, Montana, or Jackson Hole, Wyoming to get to the long dirt road that leads to it, is more than a day's round trip to visit from park headquarters.

His retirement party was a surprise party attended by over twenty people. You would think that it would be impossible to arrange a surprise party, on his last day of work, for a man who lives and works at the far end of the only road for miles. As Irvine told me later, both the party and the surprise were complete successes. "You know how Dunbar is, if there is still daylight, he thinks you ought to be working. During the day, he did hear a few more visitors coming up the road, but it being his last day, that seemed reasonable. Of course he didn't imagine not working a full day his last day, and didn't expect anyone else would imagine it either. So, when the main bunch of people came in, he was out working with his seasonals and didn't come in until almost dark."

We came back to my question about what thoughts motivated the opponents of let burn. Ted noted that we all felt that something had been taken from us when a windstorm blew down almost all the trees at "our end" of Jenny Lake. He further noted that, "because it is public land they think of it as their land." Rather than thinking of public lands as land set aside not to be owned, we think of it as being collectively owned.

We came back to animals. Said Rick, "Taking a walk in a forest that has a grizzly in it is a wholly different experience then taking a walk in one that doesn't. A very different experience. But people never think that they ought to learn to accept that threat."

Ted said that the last time he had gone bow hunting for deer they came upon elk in rut about forty yards away. They held their bows up to their foreheads, like antlers, and the elk let them crash down the dry hillside toward them. At twenty yards he pulled back on a bull. Ted sighted along an imaginary arrow for us, and then moved his bow hand back toward his body. "I pulled back and then let it down. I didn't need to kill him; getting up to him was all the thrill I needed."

We came finally to humans. The evening ended with Rick telling us about his trip through Chengdu province in China to Tibet. They traveled through areas that hadn't been visited by Europeans or Americans before. "I thought we were doing pretty well about cultural imperialism. We'd go through these valleys and people would look at our stuff in a half interested way. They were curious, but it didn't mean much to them. Our jackets were different than theirs. We had tools they didn't have, they had tools we didn't have. Our tools went with our stuff, their tools went with their stuff. Until one day in base camp the doctor took a polaroid picture of this nice young man, he was about fourteen years old. We had discussed polaroids and I had said that I thought they were a bad idea. You take one picture; then you have to take a picture of the whole village; and then you run out of film and you're bad guys. Anyway, she decided that it would be a...he was very good-looking, just the nicest looking young man...she decided it would be a nice gesture to take his picture and give it to him. So she did. The thing came out of the camera. I remember that, that was the first sign that we had a little magic. She gave it to him and he looked at the picture. It was interesting. There was a person, there were all these pretty colors. Most of the people there were old people. They got all excited. They tried to tell him that the person was himself. It made me wonder if he'd even seen a mirror before. One man in particular, maybe his uncle or granddad or something, was gesturing to him and the picture, but you could see he wasn't getting it. He had a sort of blank look. Meanwhile, while this was going on, she took a picture of him and the old guy looking at the picture. When she handed that to the young man, the color drained from his face, really, the response was physical."

"Very clever that second picture, very telling. There's not only people that take these pictures, they know what you don't know, they know how to blow your mind. Wizardry."

"Right. You could just see them thinking, 'If they can do this, what else can they do?' After that there was a definite change in the way they regarded us. We were just people like everybody else before; after the picture incident there was a distance between us. Can you imagine what it would have been if they really knew what was probably going to happen to them because of us? That may be just my interpretation but I went on and wrote about this in my journal. I asked myself what we could possibly bring them that, on balance, would make their lives better. Some medical technology, maybe. But on balance? The trouble is it all comes in a package. You can't just pull one thing out and hand it over. We had a Chinese interpreter assigned to us. I tried to talk to him about this. He said, 'Oh yes, we know about your television, and the loose ways of your young people, your Rock and Roll, but they won't affect us.' I could see what he was thinking and would have said if he wasn't being polite: 'We're over 4000 years old, do you know what we've survived in that time? How long have you been around, 200 years?' I tried to tell him that he had no idea of all that came with television, all that's inevitably attached to it. In a way, he was worse off than the people of the remote valleys because he thinks he understands technology, can hold off its unwanted effects."

The next morning I accompanied Rick Reese to his office. He was editor, publisher, and shipping clerk of Utah Geographic, a series of photographic books about Utah. There, after confirming the veracity of the salamander story, he gave me the history of the term *"the Greater Yellowstone Ecosystem."* He pulled out of his files a government document and showed it to me saying, "When I saw this, I knew we made it." The document's short title was *Committee Print No.6: Greater Yellowstone Ecosystem.* It's long title is *Analysis by Congressional Research Service, Library of Congress, For the Committee on Public Lands and the Subcommittee on National Parks and Recreation of the Committee on Interior and Insular Affairs, U. S. House of Representatives, Ninety-ninth Congress, Second Session, December 1986.* "When a government publication use a term, it's official. Inventing that term, and the idea, 'the Greater Yellowstone Ecosystem,' is probably the most important thing I have done, could be the most important thing I will do.

The idea came out of a series of evening talks I had with John Townsley, Superintendent of Yellowstone, in 1981. Townsley wasn't popular with a lot of people, but I'm one of Townsley's fans. He died in September of 1982. John had attended a hearing in Red Lodge on oil and gas leases, I think it was, on the Washakie National Forest. He stood up and said, 'Folks, I'm here, outside my park, because in my park are grizzlies with a range of hundred square miles, and I need your help; they, the grizzlies, need your help.' The very next morning after that hearing, John got a telephone call from James Watt's office calling him back to Washington. The very next day! Somebody, somebody connected to someone with big bucks, must have walked out of that hearing and called Washington at, it was a long hearing...what? two o'clock in the morning? Yeah, one or two o'clock. Townsley was told in no uncertain terms, in a meeting with Jim Watt himself, that his place was inside his park and he was not to wander outside the park boundaries again.

I talked to Townsley the evening he got back. He shook his head and said, 'I really got a reaming.' That night, and for several nights after that we had these long conversations, which led eventually to the founding of the Greater Yellowstone Coalition. I was the first chairman.

"There are besides the two parks five forests, in three separate regions, and 38 boards and commissions having jurisdiction in the Greater Yellowstone Ecosystem, and in those days, each one was a separate fieldom. One forest supervisor wouldn't discuss what he was doing with the supervisor of the forest next to him, never mind a park superintendent. Now, after only seven years, Reagan years, it is just axiomatic that the Superintendent of Yellowstone would be invited to a discussion of a thermal development in Island Park. I'm proud of that."

Possible Futures

The baby made her appearance on the 18th, in company with two other babies who showed up on the same shift in the little hospital; Jenny Leigh she is, named after the Shoshone woman who married, after the fashion of the time, Beaver Dick Leigh, who is not so much the last mountain man as the first outfitter in Jackson Hole, the first professional outdoorsman. For them, Jenny and Leigh Lakes are named. There was in the birthing a particularly interesting reminder of our ambiguous relationship to technology.

The labor went on for a while. A woman who came in later than Melanie had her baby before she did.

Connie explained what was going on to me. "That machine they had Melanie hooked up to monitors the baby's vital signs. The labor was taking longer than they liked; they really don't like it if things don't go perfectly smoothly. The monitor showed some signs of distress in the baby, naturally, being born is stressful to a baby. They had gotten false readings from that monitor recently so they weren't sure. Since Melanie wasn't all that committed to giving birth naturally anyway, they gave Melanie pitocin to induce labor. That *did* distress the baby which excited the monitor. Very few babies are allowed to be born naturally now, they are so worried about malpractice suits. They feel that with a C-Section they have more control over what happens."

I did understand that Melanie came within 90 seconds of the deadline the doctor set for giving her a C-Section.

"No more of this fancy equipment," said the doc to the nurse, "whaddya say we just do it the old fashion way from now on?"

"Okay," said the nurse, who had worked well into the next shift to deal with a crowd of babies entering the world, "that's fine with me, if we agree that there will be one nurse per mother."

"Grandma used to just grab a chunk of sagebrush in the old days," mused the doc, "but there isn't even that much sagebrush around anymore."

That was a slight exaggeration, but he had a point. In my life there has been a direct correlation between how old-fashioned the work is and how much I liked doing the work. Naturally these jobs don't pay well. In terms of job satisfaction, rangering was the second best job I ever had. The very best job I ever had was in the winter of 60/61 working on the ranch of Pete and Mary Hansen Mead south of town as a "hand" (I never achieved cowboy status). The only moments of that job that I didn't actually love involved moving an 80 ton stack of frozen hay bales from another ranch to ours. Had we done that by horse team and sleigh, as we did the feeding, I would have loved that too. Moving the hay by truck just didn't quite allow enough time to recover. The best time was the beginning of calving when Pete and I rode the herd every four hours around the clock. The temperature still was getting down to about 15 below on clear, crisp nights. I have not in all the time since seen as many stars as I did that winter, or as much moonlight on snow, nor heard the yipping and singing of coyotes so clearly. I remember in particular one guilty pleasure we had on those nights. I had recently started smoking again and Pete had recently given it up. Things were a little tight for them so Pete agreed to appear in an advertisement for Camels on horseback with the mountains in the background. For authenticity, he beat the Marlboro man all hollow (you can't tell in the picture that Pete came west from Vermont). So I switched from Pall Malls to Camels and Pete had two cigarettes a day, one on the eight p.m. ride and the other on the midnight ride—sometimes three when he was persuaded on the four a.m. ride that it was possible to have a cigarette before breakfast. I believe if I could get my job back, I'd willingly get me a pack of Pall Malls or Camels, not Marlboros, and start smoking again.

I took a drive out south of town the day before leaving. Approaching the old homestead from the back way, from the west, I was surprised to see that the house and barn were still there and the front sixty acres or so looked as they had looked. When I got closer, and could see down to the big pasture in back that bordered on the Elk Refuge, there were no cows because the pasture was full of condominiums. There's still sagebrush in the park but not much pasture left in the valley.

Learning from the Fire

On the way home I hiked up Mount Washburn, this time from Dunraven Pass. It was a beautiful fall day, sunny, cool, not much wind. It was a couple of weeks early yet for color, what color there would be in this dehydrated and then smoke cured year. There was no burn on this corner of the mountain, there were subtle shards of new green amongst the rock, bark, and duff; and the trail didn't have the usual look of beaten and scuffed into inorganic insensibility that it normally would have at the end of a summer of human appreciation. How many lives would be actually seriously altered, I wondered, just how great would be the catastrophe if we just said: "All right, closing time. Everybody out for ten years, and take all your human made food and chemicals with you. Everybody, visitors, concessioner, rangers. No, the scientists are not an exception, least of all the scientists. We do not want to hear one more word of interpretation about what's here. If it weren't for the constitution we'd forbid talk about Yellowstone. We'd confiscate everybody's slides. All we'd allow you is your memory. If after five years you remember nothing, or what you remembered could have taken place anywhere, like an argument with your spouse, then you got what you deserved. That's what this place was worth to you. You will not be coming back in at the end of the ten years." Hiking uphill without a pack permits such easy play of the mind.

My brother-in-law, Don, is a successful Jackson businessman. He has been successful not only because he knows an opportunity when he sees one. More importantly, he has the biggest heart and is quickest draw with a smile in town. All children fall totally and terminally in love with him. He talks to them as if they are people who happen to be temporarily small persons. Don just stuck around long enough for them to grow, up have more kids and start spending money in his lumberyard and hardware store. At dinner at his house the evening before, I asked Don what he would think about limiting access to the wilderness parks to those who had learned a lot about woodcraft, natural history, history, survival, and so forth. The instruction would somehow be made available to the poor as well as the rich. In the past he'd objected to a kind of environmentalist snobbery/piety, not hard to find in places like Jackson and Aspen. After a long pause, Don said he would have a problem with that, but he couldn't think of what would be better. A lottery is just a way of avoiding the issue.

The problem that Don was having, I felt certain as I moseyed up the trail, was first in having to swallow the idea of limiting access. Limited access to wide open spaces is not a concept that comes easily to a Westerner. It requires a restructuring of mind, memory, and values. Furthermore, accepting for the sake of the discussion the notion of limited access, why should he agree to the indignity of taking a test, or going to some outdoor ed school (will there be calisthenics in the morning, aerobics in the evening)? Why aren't living here, loving the place, hunting, fishing, raising a family, paying taxes, participating fully in community affairs, now and then quietly giving a hand to a person that needs it, a bit help with the tuition in the college of hard knocks—why aren't these all the qualifications a person needs? Don didn't actually have to present this question to me; I was able to think of it myself; and I didn't know the answer.

The degree to which being an outdoorsman had become a significant economic enterprise came home to me at Renny and Catherine's wedding. It was a gathering of the outdoors aristocracy. Kimbrough had characterized Renny as being "on the national register of heroes. Catherine was in effect, the managing executive of the Exum Guide Service, a position which became necessary when Glenn sold the business to a group of his former guides. Glenn was at the wedding. Eddie Exum wasn't there, Glenn told me, and neither was Chouinard because the two of them were on a fishing trip to Alaska. Almost everybody else who was anybody in the guiding, outfitting, rescuing, informing, equipping and attracting-to-Jackson's Hole trade was there. The crowd was seasoned by a batch of gray-haired men who'd been there in the valley for more than twenty-five summers. They'd earned the right to be there for reasons more than longevity. Al Read and Pete Lev told me a story about Rod Newcomb. They had some hot young rock-climbing clients. Newcomb got the job. His clients looked at this guy obviously in his forties muttering that they'd wanted to do some really hard stuff. They would have been really upset if they'd known he was fifty-five. So Rod took them out to the wall and took them up a little pitch they couldn't get up without aid. They came back thinking that they'd been climbing with one of the immortals. I loved that story.

Lev pointed Alex Lowe out to me, the young man who did the Grand Traverse. He was tall, dark, handsome, and thin, but muscular like a medium-sized pro basketball player. I declined to be introduced to him. I was beginning to feel like a museum piece. His head floating serenely above the crowd, he listened more than he talked: a man who knows what he can do but does not yet know that all eyes are marking him.

As I got higher up the trail, I saw more of what had been burning when I was last here. When the trail worked its way out to the edge of the west shoulder of the mountain, so that I could see the forest and range between Mount Washburn and Montana, I saw what had burned since I was last here. It looked like everything. The whole north side of the mountain at my feet had burned. The trees I had slipped unobtrusively through in the gully and on the ridge I had reclimbed when the firefighters turned me back, could have no longer afforded me cover. I would have been cremated in the grove where I ate lunch. I looked toward where I thought the campground was at Tower Junction. Burned, burned everywhere, burned as far as the eye could see.

To offset the inevitable exaggeration of the scope of the fire that the television pictures provided, I had, starting six miles south of the South Entrance, kept a running record of how much of the roadside was fire-scarred. This soon felt like a useless exercise in pseudo accuracy. The measurements themselves, odometer readings at forty miles per hour, had very little authority, and, even if they had been precise, their significance was entirely a matter of interpretation, as I discovered listening to the responses of people stopping at the turnouts. The ends of the response scale were, from a California car, "This isn't nearly as bad as it looked on television," and, of the same prospect, from a New Jersey car, "My God, would you look at that!" At a place overlooking the Lewis River, that to me appeared to be extensively burned, with a tin plate as a protractor, I marked off arcs of burned and unburned horizon. Only fifteen per cent was burned. That's pretty accurate, but it didn't change a whit my perception that the burn was extensive. One's eye dwells on the burned parts.

So it was with my first view from Mount Washburn. It wasn't burned everywhere, not nearly so, and most of the burn on the mountain was superficial, but there had been one helluva big fire thereabouts. Had I been there when it was burning, I would have been scared, in spite of knowing that no fire could have gotten to me if I just sat in the road near the summit where there was no fuel.

There were fires smoldering in the distance along the road to Mammoth. There were as many or more firefighters as before. What there really wasn't that much of was fuel left to burn. There was more cleanup going on than actual firefighting. The greenless landscape, the smoke abetted autumn light and spiced air, the yellow leaves here and there, "bare ruined choirs where yellow leaves, or few, or none do hang," grandfatherhood, had put me in a pensive mood. Gone soft in the fire and fall, I wasn't yet ready to leave the Rockies for a classroom full of brand new, eager eighteen-year olds. Although I had not traveled far on my way, I decided to stop in Gardiner.

The Yellowstone Mine restaurant was full of firebosses, people my age, more men than women, western folk, not a suitcoat or silk tie among them, a few western cut sportscoats, a few bolo ties. These Forest Service people wore mainly wool shirts, levis, and windbreakers, even if they did spend the afternoon in meetings. Every woman in the place old enough to be served liquor, and there were a dozen or more such women, was wearing a dress.

Waiting at the bar for a table, I decided to have a two martini meditation dedicated to Bernard DeVoto. This required persuading the bartender that I wanted true martinis, after the practice described by DeVoto in his book "The Hour": "Sound practice begins with ice. There must be a lot of it, more that the catechumen dreams, so much that the gin smokes when you pour it in. A friend of mine has said it for all time: his formula ends 'and five hundred pounds of ice.' Fill the pitcher with ice, whirl it till dew forms on the glass, pour out the melt, put in another handful of ice. Then as swiftly as possible put in the gin and vermouth, at once bring the mixture as close to the freezing point of alcohol as can be reached outside the laboratory, and pour out the martinis. You must be unhurried, but you must work fast, for a diluted martini would be a contradiction in terms, a violation of nature's order." This, the need for maximum chill, was not the point about which the bartender needed persuading; it was DeVoto's prescription for the vermouth: "There is a point at which the marriage of gin and vermouth is consummated. It varies little with the constituents, but for a gin of 94.4 proof and a harmonious vermouth, it may be generalized at about 3.7 to one." I'm not a stickler about the .7, a request for two jiggers of gin and something more than half a jigger of vermouth produces about as much incredulity in bartenders as I am willing to face. I could read her mind, "Well you never know, weathered skin, well-worn Pendleton shirt, I sure would have guessed him to be a man." I have kept the faith; it has been an easy martyrdom because every time I succeed in persuading someone to make it as Bernard DeVoto says it should be made, there is, of course, the instant gratification of a perfect martini.

My meditation was at first about my fear of what this fire season would come to mean. Wayne Williams "favored" prescribed burning. Rick opined that for political reasons if for no other, he accepted the necessity of prescribed burning. Given their views, I felt no need to have one of my own. Lord knows, the Yellowstone 99% of us sees, in no way resembles a wilderness. My guess was that the park people responsible for it would be forgiven its policy of natural regulation. When the journalists began working on their Pulitzer Prize hoping accounts of the fire, they would discover that, whatever failings there may be in the PR skills of the park researchers, there is nothing wrong either with their characters or their reason. There are no conclusive scientific reasons to not attempt natural regulation. It is doubtful that natural regulation would be allowed because our mythology says we must manage the world, there's a memo about that:

Item 1. Be fruitful

Item 2. Multiply

Item 3. Fill the earth

Item 4. Conquer it.

The Yellowstone Fires of 1988 would mark for historians, if historians there are to be after the conquest, the event at which we claimed that we were prepared to assume full responsibility for managing all of mortal existence. The hubris of it is frightening. I refuse to even imagine what the gods are going to do to us for this arrogance, which our feeling sorrowful, or bitter, or resigned, or indifferent about will not mitigate. The devoted conservator, the "environmental terrorist," the philosopher, the developer will suffer our fate equally.

Summer, who is at school agonizing because she doesn't know what to major in, used to say that she didn't expect to see thirty because somebody would have pushed the button by then. Many, probably most, of her friends would say the same thing if asked. Do they believe it? They believe it enough to be made nervous and fixated on themselves. They believe it in the way we believe any of the things we are told are true and important, in school, in books, by our parents in that tone they use when talking about the world in a general way. We believe that to say, "We live in the shadow of the mushroom cloud," is to say something true, interesting, important, but for all that not entirely real. Like redemption, it is not something we really expect to experience.

Were we to consult natural history, we might see ourselves as, like the populations of other species of animals, expanding and exploiting the environment until our population runs up against its limiting factor, which is unknown to us. We will fight the inevitability of extinction with every technological weapon we have, and will invent the story we need to do so. We will think we are making progress when our technology makes it possible to have potable water at a reasonable price. The reasonable price of potable water is, of course, any price.

Such were the thoughts of my first martini, the which made these thoughts much mellower than they may here appear to be.

Moved to my table, with my second martini, I began inviting friends into my thoughts. How could we imagine designing a different earned future? Who will we ask to give up their life first, Uncle Don, who sold the lumber that built the houses that filled up the pasture with condominiums where Pete Mead and I rode the herd in the -20°, so-cold-the-air-was-viscous, satin black, starlit midnights at the beginning of calving? Uncle Don, no more lumber for developers. The valley is so gentrified that your kids can barely afford to live here, with more than a little help from you, I suspect, and your grandchildren definitely will not be able to, unless they live in the barracks that are going to have to be built for the servant classes. Instead, you can sell cabin logs to my gray-haired climbing and ski-bumming friends, whom I do not ask how many people they have sold wilderness experiences to, how many they have addicted to mountaineering, white water, and cross-country skiing. Let us leave this subject, before we have to start calculating whose work has done the most damage, and think of Herb Swedlund, former Exum Guide, who gave it up, the cashing in on the wilderness, not too long ago.

We ran into each other at breakfast, the morning after I got back from Salt Lake, and met for lunch. Herb and Jacquot did the first ascent of the Black Ice Couloir, the most elegant ice climb in the Tetons, the first really hard ice climb in the Tetons, and the last good ice climb done before Chouinard's new axe, crampons, and combined French and Austrian techniques made cutting steps obsolete. Herb on young people, "They're awkward and distracted, wandering around like they just drank half a gallon of stump juice, weak in the hindquarters like overbred Great Danes." On Americans and wilderness. "They don't mind there being some, but they have to have their corn chips and bean dip, canned beer, and heated plastic toilet seats." On Alex Lowe, the young climber who had just done the Grand Traverse, "Oh yes, isn't he fun? He's got imagination, desire, humility, and, most of all, curiosity. You just want to be around him and watch to see what he wants to do next."

There were things that happened at the guide service: a fatality and impending lawsuits, disagreements among old friends, hasty words. Herb was criticized for bringing clients down from the Grand too fast for their enjoyment. "Not as fast as _____," responded Herb with reference to the fatality, "that's way too fast." Herb has always been quicker witted than the rest of us. Sometimes he's quicker than his best self. But none of this was why Herb stopped being a guide. There was no blame he wished to attribute to his comrades, the stickiness at the end was a sign that it was time to stop, and it's hard to end cleanly an intense relationship of over two decades. It all just went flat for him. Guiding may have gone flat for Herb, but he was as competitive as he had ever been, physically as well as mentally. On weekends he rode his mountain bike full out down mountainsides. I told Herb about how Willi Unsoeld and I had similar experiences, only Willi found he couldn't quit. Herb remembered, grinning, Willi contending with Eric Jubler on the television program "The Advocates" about how the wilderness should be used. Willi's view was that the wilderness was not public but sacred. Unsoeld's vigor made Jubler's view seem mealy-mouthed and politic. I think Willi might have said, and Herb and I would have agreed, whatever the mountains are for ultimately, producing an Alex Lowe is one good use for them. I wondered how the mountains today would have seemed to Willi. The fires, people in their fifties doing one-day ascents of the Grand, condos in the pastures, would it seem to him, as it did to me, that the mountains had shrunk?

No more martinis. One glass of red wine to go with the steak. To your health Dan. I forgive you for your offer to help me find out what was wrong with my car, me who would not use a flashlight until it appeared we could not otherwise get down before dawn, you, in so offering to help me with my car, feigning respect for my quaint aversion to technology. I forgive you because a little revenge is owed you. Some revenge you got on the hike down, when I had to give in and ask you to light the way for us, one light for the three of us because my headlamp didn't work—probably my dropping my pack fifty feet had something to do with that—the three of us, you ahead, Irene, your fairly new wife next, me stumbling along last, trying to remember the shape of the trail from what I saw of it illuminated for you and Irene, no moon, the most light from the stars, some from the Huck Fire burning on the crest of the ridge across the valley.

"Don't turn on the light, it will spoil our night vision," I had said and she agreed with me.

It had sort of been that way all day, the two of us and you. We so pointedly did not talk about old times that it must have been evident to you, and, when we were pooling our dredged up shreds of memory about the route, the ease with which the leadership passed back and forth between us. I don't doubt the depth and breadth of your liberation, admire you for it in fact, but no matter how non-chauvinistic you are about sex differences, age differences, past recreational preferences, the facts that she and I and her first husband had been climbing in these mountains when you were a child, Good Lord maybe even an infant, that she is a week older than me, and you are how much younger? that she's climbed Annapurna, "It's better with women on top" and all, the guides we met, on the way up, on the way down, at the Saddle, all gray-haired but one, remembered her, remembered me, and stole curious glances at you, all this was present all day—it could have gotten a little tiresome along about the fifteenth or sixteenth hour. She asked me to come because she might not be able to hold you in a fall, and I had been both a rescue ranger and a guide, nothing but the best for you, Dan, our regard for her is such that she can arrange these things with a hint. When we taught you to rappell, over at Blacktail Butte, you may have noticed that we were pretending to not notice your nervousness. Probably we didn't handle that well. If you were a client, we would have encouraged you to say something about it, so we could acknowledge it as normal. You did well, in fact, but had no way of knowing that. So when I had to ask you to use your light, you perked right up, chanting, "rock to the right," "rock to the left," "tree root," "water bar," again and again and again and again, guiding us you surely were. To that you had a right. Also, when we got back to the cabin and you wanted to have a beer, or a cup of coffee or some way not to end the day quite yet, I just came in, sorted out the gear, and drove to Jackson. You maybe knew that when younger we would not have ended the day so unceremoniously. There would have been at least one story of the day told to help lock our memories in. You can collect on that, too. You are one helluva good sport.

However, that's it. You are not owed for when you had to make the move off of Wall Street; when I held the rope tight, protecting you, yes, but mainly, from your point of view, not letting you move down to where it looked easier, held you when you wanted to go back, so when you tried to retreat, you transferred some of your weight to the rope and by exactly that amount the pressure of your weight on your holds was less, in effect slackening your grip on the mountain, which felt to you as if the mountain was slipping away from you. "I'm twisting," you said, the second syllable jumping into falsetto, and I did not relent or say a word, but tightened my hold on you even more for a fraction of a second, so you'd get the message that there would be no retreat, and then slacked off only enough so that you firmed up on your holds. So you had to do it or fall off—and you made the move.

"That's the most frightening thing I ever did," you said breathlessly as you scrambled up beside me. I grinned.

You may have thought, "You son of a bitch."

But probably not, you felt too good. You will never have to say you backed off or evaded the move; you did it purely. Now you know what it's all about: that very moment where you knew you were going to die, sometime anyway, and the moment that follows immediately upon that moment, where you understand that there is nobody in all creation who is more alive than you—where you realize that, for this day in your life, life itself is enough.

Owls, Tree Huggers, Timber Beasts, and Smokey: A Meditation

Spotting Owls

On Friday evening of the first weekend of June 1990, my wife and I drove down to Oregon to visit Sally and Jock, friends of ours who used to live up here in Olympia—the ladies to talk horses the gents to talk about owls, tree huggers, timber beasts, and Smokey.

Jock's job was finding and counting northern spotted owls for us—we the people—as prescribed by his employers, the U. S. Forest Service. Jock's assistants had recently spotted a new nest in an accessible place and we were planning to drive up into the mountains Saturday afternoon to see if before dark we might spot owl and nest and after dark go "hoot up" some more owls. Sally and Connie used to hangout at the same stable and Sally wanted to introduce Connie to her local stable in the morning. While they did that, Jock and I watched the Audubon Society special, *Ancient Forests: Rage Over Trees*, on his video machine.

It did not seem odd to me to begin a field trip by watching a television screen. I had been seeing spotted owls on television once or twice a week. Later in the month, during the week of its inclusion on the list of threatened species, articles with the name of the shy bird in the title appeared daily in the local and Seattle papers. The story continued after that sporadically. When someone in a logging town nailed an owl they shot to a sign, and that coincided with a lull in the president's foreign and domestic wars, the story made the paper.

Nevertheless, this is a story without a proper ending. As soon as it is no longer "the spotted owl controversy," there will be silence but no conclusion. It won't have ended; it will have merely evaporated. At the point where the antagonists withdraw into sullen silence, there will have been only rhetorical compromises: mere adjustments in the way we speak about contending positions and postures, compromises made by politicians, not by loggers and "preservationists," as the timber industry lobby has taught the loggers to term their opponents. The big corporate owners in timber industry will continue diversification into real estate development, even into recycling. The small operators will retire. The politicians will turn to other matters, newer stories, we and the story makers hoping for the mild thrill of a war or a disaster, or, if we are not to have those, at least a scandal.

Perhaps in a few years we will return to the loggers once more, to mark the passing of one more authentic lifeway. We will suffer a sentimental pang, as we do at the passing of the last old fashioned restaurant in our neighborhood. By the time we witness the death of the last northern spotted owl, in its zoological rest home, the species will have already long since slipped into extinction. The image of the owl could persist, possible a companion symbol to the passenger pigeon. The image that might linger is the television bit of the owl swooping down to take a white mouse—mice and owl both cute and innocent of our gaze hidden within the eye of the camera. The wild forest, whose demise the owl is meant to portend, is in a sense already gone— captured by designation as wilderness areas. How much longer will we be able to go into the "lovely, dark, and deep" woods of Robert Frost's imagining before they all become woodlots?

And then what?

And-then-what may be what we've already got. An image of what we have is a poster available in Northwest bookstores. "The Olympic Peninsula From Space" is a satellite view in color of the area from

Port Townsend on the top to just south of Olympia on the bottom, and from the base of the Cascades on the east to 10 miles off of Cape Flattery to the west. In the center is Olympic National Park. The picture was taken in summer, the only snow is on Mount Olympus. Encircling the snow is the rock and scree above treeline. The next ring out, from treeline down to the park boundary, is the dark green Pacific rainforest. Then there is a much wider swath of pale green second-growth flecked with the brown of bare clear-cuts, like flecks of milk-chocolate on a cupcake with lime frosting. This band consists of private timber holdings, state forest, and the Olympic National Forest. The outermost circle is open at the bottom, forming a blue horseshoe made of our waters: the deep dark blue of the Pacific and the shallower blues of (clockwise) the Strait of Juan de Fuca, Admiralty Inlet, Hood Canal and Puget Sound. Down the right margin, east of the concentric rings around Mt. Olympus, runs the almost continuous city of Everett, Seattle, Tacoma, the color of scraped deer-hide, a little interruption of green for Fort Lewis and the Nisqually Delta, with Olympia at the bottom. It is as if the brown of the urban corridor seeped westward under the waters of Puget Sound to surface as the scabrous brown patches of clear-cuts on the peninsula, perforating the private lands and public lands of the National Forest, closing in on the public lands of the National Park. What will that view be a hundred years from now, more brown of clear-cut and concrete or more green of canopied forest? Or will it be approximately what it is now? Fat chance.

I live in almost rural Olympia. New housing developments have approached to within a mile and are closing in on us from two directions. During the past five years new houses have been built in the developments a mile south of us at the rate of fifty per year. The Chehalis Western no longer carries carloads of logs through the pasture behind our pasture down to Woodard Bay, or anywhere else in the county. The county commissioners are at this moment planning the Chehalis Western Trail, the "management plan to include an equestrian trail," which will be nice for us, but makes the neighborhood something of a cross between abandoned dairy farms and Central Park.

Still, two-thirds of our two acres *is* pasture; across the road from us there's a one-hundred and twenty acre swamp, still so natural that it has not yet been elevated to wetland; and there are but five houses on the two hundred acres east and south of us. We are beyond the suburb but not really rural. The suburb is spreading out from a sub-stantial medical complex which includes St. Peters Hospital and the large HMO, Group Health. Half a mile south of us lives our friend the pediatrician farmer. Two miles north of us lives our friend the surgeon farmer. A fair land-use designation for the South Bay-Johnson Point-Hawks Prairie area of Thurston County would be "wannabe-rural."

Down the road a quarter of a mile in the direction of the creeping developments, on a strip of high ground between the swamp and the road, sits a trim bungalow, it and its driveway nested within another, wider, semi-circular driveway, into which a big expensive logging truck enters dusty or muddy in the evening and emerges from, washed clean, in the morning. On the northernmost tree of this property is nailed a sign—faced toward me as I see it—that says "This family supported by timber dollars." With no sign, I support preserving habitat for the spotted owl. However, since I support what he sees as a threat to his way of life—the same way of life as mine in where and how we live when we are not at work, and since it is not consequential to him that I wish to support *him* without supporting the timber industry—I believe I owe it to my logger neighbor to at least know what a northern spotted owl looks like off camera.

Our final preparations for doing that were to go the ranger station to sign releases and to pick up some mice to feed the owls, then to stop at Kentucky Fried Chicken to pick up feed for us.

While we were thus making preparations for our field trip into the primeval forest, Sally told us about when she and Jock took Jock's visiting parents to a local cafe, right there in the middle of logging country. Jock's mom, understandably proud of her son's work as an owl seeker and protector, began speaking of his work in a voice that could easily be heard at the neighboring tables. Jock signed for silence with all the body language at his command. This was a tricky operation. What people in the cafe would think about his work if they heard her, and what *their* body language might express, was the least of Jock's discomfort. With them was an old friend of the family who retired from the Forest Service recently. Jock didn't know how the old friend felt about changes that had been taking place within the service, changes toward diminishing the importance of timber sales. Had their friend been counted among the Timber Beasts in the service, as those are called who believe that the service's overriding function is to provide a sustained supply of raw logs, or was he one who had come to believe that their chief responsibility was to maintain a forest? Thanks to Jock's mom they soon discovered that their friend was one of the loyal career foresters who had watched the overcutting of the past two decades with sadness and alarm. He and Jock had an intense conversation about the future of the Forest Service and what is left of our virgin forests.

Provisioned with live mice and dead chicken we climbed into a government Blazer and headed into the Cascades. We climbed through the checkerboard of old and new clear-cuts alternating with stands of uncut forest. The boundaries between cut and uncut patches are often straight lines that appear curved to the eye as they slice across a hogback or loop down into a drainage. The lines appear straight or curved, hard or soft, according to the angle of the sun and the viewpoint of the observer. No clear-cut ever looks like it belongs where it is. Whether it is perceived to be a process of production or destruction is a matter of perspective, both psychological and political.

An hour after we started up into the Cascade foothills, Jock parked the Blazer on one of the platforms at the top of a clear-cut in the middle of old growth. In less than ten minutes we were watching a northern spotted owl. Even Jock was surprised to have so easily found the owl, and delighted. He had not been able to find an accessible owl for his parents. With The Controversy building, Jock anticipated that there might be some important visitors to his district who would happily take a look at a drive-in spotted owl. I didn't take it as a slight to my woodlore skills that we started with a drive-in owl. After dark we were going be hooting for owls. I couldn't imagine Jock inviting any VIP's to do that.

Because only nesting pairs are protected, the main purpose of our trip was not to spot another owl, but to try to determine whether or not this already spotted owl had babies. The way to do that is to give the owl a mouse and follow her as she takes it to her young. If she doesn't take it to her young that means either that she doesn't have any owlets or that her owlets are well-fed at the time—or so logic might suggest. By the transcendent set of rules governing the game of spotting spotted owls, if there are no owlets, then the owl is not in owl habitat; and if two people don't see the owlet then the spotted owl had neither habitat nor owlet. If any of the virgin forest is preserved, be assured that it isn't because we were duped by a few unscrupulous soft-on-owls indifferent-to-humans biologists.

Feeding the mouse to the owl was the easy part. Jock fished a mouse out of the bucket by its tail, held it up in clear view of the owl, and put it on a log. The owl flew down and plucked the mouse off the log. The bird's wing-span was about the same as mine; she flew past me a wing span away with not a whisper of a feather from those great wings. I knew about the owl's frictionless flight, but that had not prepared me for the weirdness of experiencing it. Hearing is not nearly as important a sense to humans as our bifocal sight, but it is about all we have to protect our backside. Not being able to hear an animal that big that close isn't right.

Noiseless flight was one aspect of the eerie experience of her silent, speedy descent from her perch to the mouse, the other was her lack of caution. I would have been inclined to pity her if I hadn't realized that she had no fear of us not because she thought we were harmless, but because we were literally insignificant to her, unworthy of notice. In all of the hundreds of thousands of years in which our ancestors shared this planet, her ancestors never had to pay any mind to ours. Whereas we have a number of old stories about owls, the spotted owl, whose stories are writ in its behavior, has no stories about us. We, in nervous compulsion to assert our self-importance, characterize this media/political skirmish as owls vs. people, while the owl can not deign to notice us. Spotted owl language has no word for people. Our ancestors must not have amounted to much in the primeval forest.

If forest service biologists carrying buckets of mice keep visiting their nesting sites, northern spotted owls will have, if not a story about us, at least an anecdote. That might be comforting, a first step toward creating an animal that is almost as happy to see us as our dog. If we domesticate the spotted owl maybe we can avoid thinking about what is most eerie about killing off species whose members refuse to acknowledge that we exist. The implication of their not being able to notice us to our reading of the moral of the most important story of all, the creation story, is chilling. The big issue of the creation story is, of course, whether God created the earth to suit us, or created us to suit the earth. This is an issue whether the creation was done by natural or supernatural forces. It is an issue whether we favor the "master and subdue" or the steward version of Genesis. Our insignificance to spotted owls has to mean that God did not create the forest to suit us but to suit the owl. Or, God created the owl to suit the forest. Either way we are in trouble because, if God created the owl to suit the forest, God did not think it vital for the owl to note the existence of our species: suggesting that God created neither us nor the forest for the other. If God created the forest for both, the owl and humans, why are we destroying both the forest and the owl? Jealousy? Not a promising view of our species. I suppose there could be people who think that God created the forest and the owl for us to destroy, but if we are that exalted, the spoiled and willful brats of a god, gods or goddesses whose delight is the spectacle of our destroying the companions we have been given to play with, what would be the point of creating a creature that ignores us? How is our species exalted by eliminating species to whom we are invisible? If David killed Goliath by hitting him with a rock dropped through the windshield of his Cadillac from a freeway overpass, would we think him exalted? Would God? There are people who say that God doesn't care about any of us, folks, owls, trees, or forests. It is difficult to refute that assertion. Fortunately, since my point is that we are in trouble, and the view that God is indifferent to all of us is not inconsistent with my point, there is no need for me to make the attempt.

Logger Image

Except for the owl, who persists in acting as if nothing we do is of any consequence, all of the talkers in this discourse agree that we are in trouble: timber industry, loggers, forest service, environmental extremists and politicians. Reporters—for whom there is the problem and then there is the problem of with a straight face presenting the problem as if a solution could be imagined—have doubled trouble.

The positions are clear in this contention over the last of the aboriginal forest. Tree huggers would not cut another ancient tree from a virgin forest, timber interests would cut all the "over mature" trees and convert old growth to "productive forest." Both sides want all the virgin forest that is left. Neither side really expects to win it all, but neither is there a middle ground. Most citizens, especially those east of the 98th meridian, believe that places like Olympic National Park are set aside in perpetuity. Loggers who live in the encircling towns assert that timber in the park is only temporarily "locked up." The loggers have the stronger position. The only certainty that we won't cut those trees later would be in cutting them sooner. As the Western story of free and practically unlimited resources yields to the "New Story" of the American West of declining and priceless grass, timber, fish, potable water, clean air and space, westerners will continue their century and a half old admonition that the federal government help us to develop "our" resources and then stay out of the way as we privately maximize the monetary value of these resources, blaming the government for what we've done wrong, of course.

In those cozy homes of loggers that the owl is threatening to destroy—scattering the family after a bout of substance abuse, wife and child abuse, and maybe even suicides, as one version of the story goes—are television sets, more of them paid for than you might think by how the story goes.[1] We know that, however simple the life of a logger may be, going out in the woods every day to cut and haul trees 'cause they got kids to raise, there ain't no loggers so simple as not to

---

1. Bob Partlow, "In FORKS, it is not an owl. It is a story about PEOPLE," The Olympian, Sunday, 2 June 1991

know that the way to a politician's heart is through his television set. Loggers are not a whit less self-conscious of their image than (in declining order of respectability) cowboys, cops, street people, or politicians.

Loggers know that they not only give the reporters their human interest angle, the way logger's live their lives provides the authenticity of the story. Would you believe it? There are people who actually make a living by going out in the woods, walking up to a tree and falling it. Then choker setters, younger men, brave, but not-so-skilled as the cutters, attach a cable to the felled tree so it can be dragged up the mountainside to be loaded on a truck. There are all-women tree-planting crews in the Northwest, restoring life in the wake of the chain saws. Loggers wear high-topped "corked" boots; cut-off, high-water pants with suspenders; and the checkered shirts with the bold indiscrete checks. Logger's boots are utterly unlike cowboy boots in that logger's boots are still so exclusively used for the purpose for which they were designed, that, as I have said, for me they lend the conclusive touch of authenticity to the garb of smokejumpers.

Logging is not only honest work, it is one of very few occupations that can honestly be called physically hard work. Work that is as physically demanding as is logging makes us nostalgic for a simpler life. Any work that is as physically dangerous as is logging commands the kind of respect that makes us want to savor our nostalgia only, not do it. Connie was for several years an emergency room nurse down the road, the emergency room to which loggers on the west coast of Washington from the Olympic Peninsula south to the Columbia River are transported when they are seriously injured. Logging is second only to riding a motorcycle on the first sunny day in spring as a sure-fire way to get badly hurt. Although chainsaw cuts are some of the worst wounds she dealt with, these rarely happen to loggers. Chainsaw wounds happen to suburban husbands getting in the wood for their fireplace inserts and wood stoves. Loggers tend to be crushed by tree trunks, branches, cables, and heavy machinery. Loggers have ranked over cowboys, roughnecks, and motorcycle toughs on Connie's toughness scale ever since a logger came into the emergency room who had fallen out of the bed of a pick-up going thirty miles an hour on a gravel road, thus bearing motorcycle-type injuries. She spent half a shift scrubbing embedded gravel out of his skin with a stiff brush. It took so long because she couldn't brush while laughing at his jokes.

Paradoxically, loggers are so authentic that they are in danger of being transmuted to legend. Indeed this fight would be a lot more fun for environmentalists if it could be fought out between the environmental lobbies, the wood products corporations, the bureaucracy of the forest service, political appointees managing the Departments of Agriculture and Interior, and the elected politicians. All of the opponents of clear-cut logging of old growth forests that I've talked to regard the loggers themselves as more the victims of the system than the parties responsible. Environmentalists are reluctant to criticize loggers, or to say much of anything about them. The position of environmentalists is analogous to that of the narrator of Robert Frost's "Two Tramps in Mud Time" when two loggers come upon the narrator splitting wood:

> Nothing on either side was said.
> They knew they had but to stay their stay
> And all their logic would fill my head:
> As that I had no right to play
> With what was another man's work for gain.
> My right might be love but theirs was need.
> And where the two exist in twain
> *Theirs was the better right—agreed.*

Sympathy makes your opponents feel uncomfortable, but sympathy is not easily converted to effective political power, and I suspect that the loggers didn't try to. The bumper sticker is the logger's equivalent of the sound bite, "Spotted Owl Tastes Like Chicken," and homemade signs over the back counters of cafes, "I love Spotted Owl Fried in Exon [sic] Oil."

These, though seen by fewer people, have more staying power than newspapers and television. By these means the issue is effectively characterized as "owls versus . . ." variously: people, jobs, homes, or families, just as environmentalists feared would happen back in 1976 when the northern spotted owl was made the indicator species for the health of the forests. What environmentalists did not foresee is how effectively loggers have made their case known. What loggers might not have foreseen is how little but sympathy their story can generate.

Because the loggers live far from our television transmitting facilities here in the Northwest, we have gotten their story mainly from the papers. The reporters took us out into the woods with fourth generation cutters who explained what they do, speaking of the danger only aslant if at all. In town, the wives talk of family and community and surviving the down-cycle of the boom and bust industry they and their antecedents have worked in since the Yankees Pope and Talbot set up their mill in Port Gamble in 1853—as well as a Congregational Church. The latter proved to be the more enduring of the two.

The other kind of story was not set in the woods or in the kitchen, but at a "rally," as editorially approved demonstrations are called these days. Bill Pickell, general manager of the Washington Contract Loggers Association, said that loggers, truckers and mill workers had been "lined up to go to the concentration camps," by environmentalists; "and the politicians are lined up right behind them scheduling the trains." (He said this at a rally in Hoquium in April of 1991 scheduled to coincide with a celebration of bird watchers at nearby Bowerman Basin. The bird watchers canceled.) Then he gave them an effigy of Congressman Jim Jontz of Indiana to burn. At the same rally, Larry Mason who owns Mason Lumber Products, told the crowd, "You better be registered to vote. You better be ready to talk. You better be ready to get in the way because if you're not you're going to get run over." Earlier he is reported to have asked rhetorically, "What are we supposed to do? Lay down and get pissed on by the urban population?"[2] On the day the Fish And Wildlife Service announced that it would list the owl as threatened, a timber worker was quoted as observing, "There won't be any old growth in the Olympic National Park if someone burns it down."[3]

These little attention getters worked. The public and the politicians were listening and watching. The loggers had their moment.

2..Brad Shannon, "Thousands block bridge, denounce spotted-owl plan," The Olympian, Sunday, 29 April 1990.

3..Larry Werner, "Tension builds in logging community," Seattle Post-Intelligencer, Saturday, 23 June 1990.

What could they do with it? While it may be true that a picture is worth a thousand words, it does not follow that a couple of picturesque phrases are worth a thousand words. They can be, the phrases of poets are, but there are some issues in political discourse that require quite a few thousand carefully picked and placed words. In the battle of the timber industry lobby versus the environmentalist lobby, loggers, by putting themselves in the forefront of the public relations battle, set themselves up to take the fall.

When the Northwest timber delegation went to the other Washington to talk to John Sununu, they were told that their strategy had to be to get better at getting their story out to the public.[4] That was amusing. If the timber representatives didn't already know that, and hadn't been at least partly successful at it, they wouldn't have been having a thirty-minute meeting at the White House. The meeting with John Sununu was itself news. Their complaint instantly ranked among those that have to be listened to. Its cost to loggers was that they thus allowed themselves to be cast as victims. They also made themselves the front line troops of their old adversary, the timber industry. In the midst of a recession, when many people lost their jobs and fear for the welfare of their families, loggers left themselves two choices for enemies, the northern spotted owl or the environmental movement, neither of whom can be accused of having economic motives. Persuading us that the owl and the Sierra Club are responsible for our falling behind Japan and the Europeans is a hard sell. Persuading us that this is a conflict between plain wholesome country folk and effete, snobbish urban folk, who like their scenery to be green, is easier, but only if they believe it themselves will it not sound hollow.

Loggers know that their era is past but can't say it to themselves. In one newspaper story a woman was quoted as saying, "We only cut what the government lets us cut, and now they say we've over-cut."[5] This woman is a country person. She lives out there. Can't she see the clear-cuts? Not as we do. Loggers hang on to sustainable yield as an article of faith as fiercely as a convent novitiates hang on to the story

4. John Teare, "Bush aide hears logging plea," The Olympian, Friday, 15 June 1990.

5. "Horns blaring, angry loggers parade through Roseberg, Ore." Seattle Times/Seattle Post-Intelligencer, Sunday, 24 June 1990.

of immaculate conception. The novitiates have a somewhat better chance of not getting screwed. For sustained yield to work, fifty percent or more of the forest has to be fifty percent or more on the way to maturity. If the forest being managed is on a 70 year sustainable yield plan, half the trees have to be 35 years old or older. In the past twenty years, right in full view of everybody, country girl and city boy alike, a percentage of the forest that looks to be a lot more than fifty percent has been cut. Only shreds of the forest are left. It doesn't take a statistician to figure out that this rate of cutting is not sustainable.[6]

Furthermore, what the country girl knows and most city boys don't know is that this great cut of the past two decades was accomplished with fewer and fewer men. Even if the timber industry, with the help of sympathy for loggers, won everything that is left, everything that is left will be cut by still fewer men. The log dumps of the ports in this area, in anticipation of reduced quotas, are as full as they would be in boom times. No matter what happens, there will be fewer loggers in the woods. There are certainly no fourth generation loggers who don't know this.

The history is that the timber barons, who put together vast tracts of land we usurped from the sustainable use of the indigenous peoples and animals, cut over all their privately owned land and then managed to persuade the forest service that its function was not to protect the forests but jobs and communities, which it could do by selling public trees to them at a very good price. Now that the public forests are almost out of "product," as well as owls, all responsibility for jobs and communities has fallen to us, the public. Timber Beasts in the state and national forest services and in the land management bureaus, such as the United States Bureau of Land Management and the Washington State Department of Natural Resources, the loggers, and the politicians turn to us and ask us if, by means of the Endangered Species Act, we seriously choose to have exotic animals nobody ever gets to

6. For example, the following by Richard W. Larsen, associate editor of The Seattle Times, Sunday, 24 June 1990:

For hundreds of thousands of other Washingtonians, those denuded mountainsides along Interstate 90, across Snoqualmie Pass—the clearcutting done on Plum Creek's vast holdings, on public forests, other lands—became a 30-mile long-billboard that flashes an emotion-heating message about logging excesses... cutting trees at twice the rate that the forests can regenerate.

see, rather than good country people, out here in the western forests? A yes answer to that question is how you get to be an environmental extremist.

The history of the West has been a massive experiment in combining socialist economic principles with a myth of the American Adam as a heroic rugged individualist. (Eve is here too, without the serpent, without anybody to talk to, in fact, except her old man.) The American Adam is a man who complains constantly about two things, government interference and that the government hasn't outfitted his garden properly—he wants ever more free land, mineral rights, timber rights, and water. What does the public get in return for this socialism absent any principle of justice? The implication is clearly that what we get is virtuous folks. How virtue is supposed to bloom, when the Daddy Adam is a creature who is either in a rage or whining, is still being worked out.

Tree Hugging

Although I am a recent convert to environmental extremism, I am a long time sojourner in desert places.

Since visiting the Greater Yellowstone Ecosystem during the fires of 1988, where the political consequences of policies attempting to leave the forests alone first earnestly occupied American television screens, I found ways to get into virgin forests in Washington, Oregon, and the Tongass National Forest in Southeast Alaska. I went there for recreation and to learn more about what is at stake in the effort to prevent the complete loss of these last ancient forests.

Who has the right to be there has been a personal concern since I was a seasonal national park ranger during the sixties, watching the Grand Teton National Park begin to disintegrate under the crush of visitors brought there by a huge NPS public relations effort. It has been still a concern since I became no longer a ranger but myself a visitor. Establishing the moral, or at least more-than-merely-legal, right to be where we are has been an American topic since colonization. Now aware of the capacity of our species for self and environmental destruction, our right to inhabit the planet is itself in question.

Americans are well positioned by history and geography to contemplate this question. We all came to the New World from somewhere else. There are two choices, we make a place our place either by seizing possession of it or by earning a right to be there. The trouble with seizing a place is that there is no logical end to it. Others may do as we have done with right equal to ours. That is why we still, after having seized the land, wish to establish a right to it.

Having a right to our land, ours because of ownership, or ours because we are from there, or in some other way belong there is one of our values. Obtaining clear moral title, however, is such an uncertain matter that it probably accounts for the continuance of Social Darwinist thought in America. We are here because Nature has determined that we are fit to be here. That same ideological train of thought accounts for our public poverty—particularly in the West are we reluctant to make and do magnificent public work, tangible or intangible. Valuing community work of the highest order would interfere with the natural processes whereby our personal fitness for our weal is revealed. Thus loggers are uneasy about proposals to help them out. On the one hand they feel they personally did nothing to deserve ruin, but accepting help is evidence that they weren't fit to hold their places.

There are other metaphysical manifestations of our hidden fear that the Great Bartender beyond space is thinking about calling for the bouncer to pitch us out of this party. Underlying the notion that the settlers were entitled to the lands they usurped if they improved them is an awareness of the hubris of claiming the power to improve the creation. Western politicians are twisting themselves up in legal snarls trying to invent legal weapons against that don't too obviously give the lie to their prostestations of valuing freedom above all. All us white folks know that Mexicans preceeded us as conquerors, as aboriginals or both. They are not immigrants.

Whether the loggers on the Olympic Peninsula have earned the right to be there or not, they have more right than do I because they have the highest sanction we can provide: they make their money that way. It is a truth self-evident in our tradition that "the pursuit of happiness" means making good money, if indeed it isn't also the case

that liberty means freedom to make money by any means not specifically forbidden by statute, and life means the good life as measured
by disposable income. I have colleagues—biologists, naturalists, ecolo-
gists, natural historians—who are paid to sojourn in the wilderness. I
have other friends who are committed amateur naturalists. Their
knowledge gives them title to the wild places. I am none of these, I am
at best a fan of those who spend their lives thinking about nature in a
technical way. When I go into the wild, I don't read the landscape as
do my friends, calling latin nouns from memory. I am very attentive
to the big bears, (*Ursa horribilis* or "grizzlies" as the upland members of the brown bear species are called). I pine for stories and information about them, particularly their interactions with the species I
am mainly interested in, us.

On my excursions to the ancient forests, loggers have been ever at
the periphery of my vision. Even in Alaska it is not easy to find a
section of old growth large enough so that you can't see a clear-cut
from the water or a mountain top. It can be done if you use a float
plane or an helicopter to get far enough away, but it seems like cheating to visit by means of expensive technology a patch of earth that is
as created. It is impossible to be a purist about this. The logic of the
line I draw I would be embarrassed to try to defend to one of my
philosophical or mathematical friends. It works by feel. It was okay
to take the train to Talkeetna to climb Denali in 1959. I wish we
hadn't flown in to the glacier. Since we did fly in, I'm glad it was with
the legendary pilot, Don Sheldon. It feels better to sin in company
with a legendary figure, like being caught outside of Madonna's apart-
ment building in the wee hours.

By means of a fiberglass kayak—which means that from the point
of view of loggers and timber beasts, I forfeit the right to deplore
their "use" of our ancient national forests—I do manage to get out of
sight of clear-cuts in Alaska. I myself am not pleased to see other
kayakers up there, especially those that plan to write stories about it
for *Sea Kayaker* encouraging others to join the fun—not pleased because I feel guilty, not possessive. I have seen what we portend. To a
person in love with the world as God made it, there's little to choose
between clear-cuts and golf courses, except that clear-cuts seem more

honestly pushed in faces of the gods. Loggers are willing to live with the places they exploited.

Loggers say they can't be anything but loggers. It's not just that they don't want jobs serving hamburgers to teenagers at minimum wage; loggers don't want to live anywhere but in places where everybody knows logging, knows the stories. When asked if they couldn't find other work they respond, sometimes a little impatiently, "What would I do?" meaning not only why me, really meaning that there is no other work that most loggers would find worth doing.

Robert Payne, the trade books manager in our bookstore, was once a logger. We had a conversation about his logger days. He began logging while in high school, working summers in his uncle's gypo logging outfit, went to Viet Nam, and, after his return from Viet Nam, got a job on a Simpson Timber crew doing high lead logging in the foothills and lower slopes of the Olympics.

Is Robert an authentic logger? One of my colleagues with ties to a logging family, says not. His view is that one of your grandfathers had to have done it, an uncle won't do. Also, there can't have been any choice, you log because that's all you and all the people important to you do. Probably my colleague is technically right in the sense he means it, but there was, in Robert's view, no choice about trying it. "I have to see for myself. I have to experience it. It was the same for Viet Nam." What he saw in Viet Nam was that they were asking him to pay too high a price for the fun of it. That's also what he found to be the case about logging.

High lead logging is an example of a technical innovation coping with a diminishing resource, or, as we used to say, necessity is the mother of invention. When there were no more big trees to log on the flats, in the river bottoms, off the gentler hills, and off the steep slopes falling directly into the Sound, the timber companies turned to the mountain sides. Logs are no longer gotten out of the mountains by river, flume, or log train. How is a downed tree removed from a slope so steep that even a slight tug on a cable would be enough to roll the bulldozer all the way to the bottom? Logs are moved from the clearcut, a handful at a time, one log at a time if they are old growth, by logging trucks driving down a logging road. The trees are moved from where they were felled by suspending them from a cable and hauling them uphill against gravity. Bull dozers aren't used for hauling logs but to build the road for the trucks and the platform for the tower from which the cable leads downhill. The tower replaces the spar of former times. The log is always under control, if nothing goes wrong. The likely places for something to go wrong are when hooking the log up to the cable and when releasing it from the cable.

Robert's job, memorably called "whistle-punking," was to give the signal to release the suspended log when he thought it was safe to do so. His job could be thought of as the safety officer at the tower. Because he had to think about the trade-off of speed and safety, Robert was in a position of potential conflict with the crew boss. The crew boss's job was to whirl his finger in a circle over his head, the signal for "highballing," which is to loggers what "showtime" was to the L. A. Lakers in the days of Kareem, Magic, and Pat Riley. Robert worked from June 1975 to February 1976, the winter shutdown, didn't return with no regrets either about having done it or quitting.

Had he had regrets they would have been for giving up the life. Work hard all day, full out, to stay in shape for the drinking and loving at night. Athletes, day and night. He has a clear memory of a footrace of the whole crew down the mountainside at the end of one day, his buddy, thirty-six years old at the time like himself, hanging right in there with the twenty-year-olds, leaping and dodging, laughing and yelling. There are very few jobs that will give you so much life. Of the jobs I've tried, mountain guide, ski patrol, oil field roughneck, none quite compare. Mountain rescue comes close, but it's too sporadic. Cowboying comes closer, but the pay was so bad that it was like life on a plantation with a humane master. Of jobs I haven't tried, smoke jumping is the job I most regret not having tried. Commercial fisherman is second. Smoke jumping is clearly better than logging. Trolling for salmon is probably not, because it is not athletic enough, but I would rather do it because salmon are a renewable resource, theoretically at least, trees twice as old as the nation are not practically renewable, and a forest is not even theoretically renewable in less than the span of a civilization.

Robert has another clear memory from those days: an image of an older logger staring at his favorite place in the forest, a place that they were about to cut over, shocked into recognition that it wasn't the society, the economy, our way of life, or the industry that made of a forest a wasteland of stumps, slash, exposed dirt, and Fireweed—or maybe it *was* those things in the big picture—but, when it got right down to it, it was he who would start up the unpitying saw. It was all necessary, he knew that, more than necessary, a matter of survival. The life of every logger is a matter of survival, no whining, exulting survival. The logger took it on trust that the same was true in the larger world, some folks with better work than logging, most not, everybody doing what they had to do to get by. It might be less clearly a matter of survival for some than it is with him. There was no pride in that, perhaps he couldn't do well with the subtleties of survival in town; he's happy to learn from TV how people live in the city. Nothing inferior about urban life, it's just not how loggers do.

Has that logger, fifteen years later and, if he survived, retired now, been persuaded to join in with the whining? It's all about families, is how the story goes, "This family is supported by the timber industry," reads my neighbor's sign. He has another one, the other side of the deal, "We support the timber industry." Loggers in tight with the timber industry: very different from the early days of this century, the days of the IWW strikes of protest against conditions in the camps. In 1917 the Wobblies shut down logging on the Pacific Coast.

"Loggers are an endangered species," says the T-shirt. The opposition also has access to the people's media, "If loggers, are an endangered species," says the reply, "it isn't because owls mismanaged their habitat."

"Try wiping your ass with a spotted owl," the logger replies, playing hardball.

A logger knows about moss. The old logger is willing to speak up to urban folk, in cahoots with his former adversary the timber industry. For political reasons, he is willing to keep quiet about the moss: that it grows only on the spacious floor of the multi-canopied old growth forest, not in crowded second growth tree plantations, and certainly not in clear-cuts. It's not only urban folk but the loggers too who'll be needing substitutes for toilet paper *and* moss.

The logger will also keep quiet about the miracle. The miracle is that the miserable, meager, 90% rock and 9% red clay, poor excuse for soil, an embarrassment when exposed by the bulldozer blade making a road, or the log swiping the ground cover off as it is snatched into the air after the chokers have been set—the miracle is that out of the 1% of fecund organic material, something as magnificent as straight grain, close grain, clear grain cedar, fir, hemlock, or spruce lifts itself into the sky. The logger keeps quiet about the moss because he is to that degree willing to be in cahoots with the timber industry and its spokesperson's stories. He keeps quiet about the magnificent trees because he could never make himself believed if he tried to explain how he loves those trees while he falls them. It's the same about hunting. The only love urban people understand is sentimental love, pretty love. The love that comes from clear-eyed participation in one's own mortality urban people don't want to hear about. The logger would have no difficulty understanding what the point is of a bullfight.

The family and community stuff isn't all hype. Robert regrets not having lived in one of the camps. The timber industry succeeded in destroying the IWW, and then went ahead and cleaned up the camps, as had been demanded. Wives and children were included. The camps had their own schools. The last one, Camp Grisdale, closed only eight years ago. The life must have been the last surviving spirit of the paleolithic village in the Lower Forty-eight, a commune of plaid-shirted, tobacco chewers. Young loggers carried through the seventies and eighties to the present the long hair of the hippies and a form of imaginative functional dress of their own.

Robert left the industry partly because of highballing, partly he too was alarmed to see how quickly they could strip a hillside. Together it added up to something it seemed he ought not to be doing. He'd already learned about war. You don't have to know precisely what is wrong to know it isn't right. When I asked Robert what in his view went wrong he replied, "When the old timers who cut the trees with axes and two-man saws, 'misery whips' they called them, looked at the forest, they must have really thought that we could never cut it all. It was the invention of the power saw that made it possible to cut it all."

The Discourse on Disaster

The way it works in a story determined to be about a disaster is that some of us have to be victims, the reporter assumes the role of concerned citizen and the rest of us get the job of being insufficiently conscious of the gravity of the event and the plight of the victims—or worse, loving the excitement. The lineaments of this genre were worked out during the Yellowstone Fires of '88.

That was when I started monitoring my responses to both television and newspapers. There are people who would have responded differently. Around town I see a bumper sticker that says "Shoot Your Television." I prefer a Ghandian approach and merely abstain from watching television for weeks at a time (the weather channel excepted). The price for this is that the feeling that I am missing something becomes a craving. When I get this childish feeling of not being included, I binge on TV and read as much news as I can stand. Remorse then follows. I ask myself what I have learned. I end up with a feeling that I have seen what is happening, I wasn't tricked, but I still think I don't know what is going on. I don't like the feeling.

So it is with disaster stories. I am more of a black hat than a white hat in this owl vs. logger thing. It was the same in the story about the Yellowstone fire. There I was in good company. Park officials were suddenly transformed from protectors of the wilderness to—worse than indifferent to the destruction of our most venerable and sacred park—the actual perpetrators of the "environmental disaster." Those park folks had major image trouble. Smokey the Bear has been teaching us to fear and morn forest fires since 1946. While the once-singed bear is a creature of the U.S. Forest Service, his hat is that of a National Park Service ranger. Smokey-hatted rangers allowing forest fires to burn transmitted more static than the park's public relations squelch knobs could mute.[7]

Environmental disaster is a kinder, gentler sub-genre of the larger news genre, disaster-as-entertainment. The parent genre is made up of

7.. Amy Vanderbilt, telephone conversation 24 October 1988.

events where people are killed, such as Bophal and Chernobyl. Environmental disaster belongs to the Discovery Channel not CNN. The *Exxon Valdez* oil spill was the environmental disaster story of the next year, 1989. That story was something of a reprieve of those of my ilk, the environmental extremists of the Yellowstone fire era. The concerns of environmental extremists seemed less crank in the context of the destruction of wild and distant beaches by a captain in his cups, a novice at the helm and computer error, all common experiences to many of us.

The oil spill established a place for wilderness in the environmental disaster genre in a way that the Yellowstone fire could not. Although most of us do know that fire is not really a disaster to nature but natural goings-on in an ecosystem, Yellowstone is too domesticated, Central Park scaled up to western size, to stand for wilderness. When we learned that very few large animals died in the fire, we were left with a fire in a theme park in which there was no structural damage, just more black and less green in the landscaping. Nostalgia was the principle emotion, the evacuation of guests of Old Faithful Inn the principle drama.

The threat of urban human culture to wild nature appeared clearer in the case of the *Exxon Valdez* oil spill than it was in the Yellowstone story. As a matter of ecological fact, however, humans had done far more damage to the Greater Yellowstone Ecosystem than the fire did or our oil could do to Prince William Sound. The oil killed many individual organisms and undoubtedly somewhat reduced the carrying capacity for many species in the area, but the spill extinguished no species. It did damage the image of Prince William Sound. We can no longer think of it as pristine.

What was most satisfying about the Valdez oil spill is that in the boozed-up captain it served us up a scapegoat, and Exxon does nicely as villain. In the case of the fires of 1988, we could be sold on the notion that the Park Service was inept, or too rigid in its environmentalism, but it was very hard to make out the Park Service to be villainous. How much more pleasing it was to discover that our big trouble is the fault of large multinational corporations, deep-pocketed corporations who can be sued for serious money, a beautiful waterfall in the wilderness of trickle-down economic policy. It is sometimes a just world after all.

The Gulf War's addition to the genre was of prime importance. Saddam Hussein knew he was creating a spectacle with the burning of Kuwait's oil. It is plausible that he had no thought for the wild creatures that were killed. He was surprised and delighted to find that we were outraged by the images of oil-slicked cormorants. As we got the images of soldiers, helicopters, and walls of flame in Yellowstone to remind us vaguely of the Viet Nam War—the *ur* disaster, encompassing dreadful consequences: political, environmental, social, economic, and moral—we got reminded again in the images of the Gulf War. Only this time it wasn't an analogy.

Both the Yellowstone Fire story and the *Exxon Valdez* story contained little stories about what would now, post Gulf War, be called "collateral damage": outfitters and gift-shop owners whining about how tough this is gonna be on them in the former, and fisherman whose season was ruined in the Prince William Sound story. Nobody local to the area except information officers in the park listened to the concessionaires in Yellowstone area, and there were Alaska fishermen aplenty sufficiently willing to let Exxon buy them off to have cleaned up in the clean-up.

I don't know how the people in Atlanta take these vignettes, but collateral damage, though now a formal requirement of the environmental disaster genre, is unconvincing in all cases except those like Mt. Saint Helens, where people actually die.

The family fighting to preserve the contended valley of old growth in the *Ancient Forests: Rage Over Trees* story owns a recreational cabin at the head of the valley, the value of which must be incalculable—a point that is muted in the video but not lost to the audience. Near the end of that story called rage, we get interviews with a group of people who, as they are shown on their hands and knees working on a trail, could be the local garden club.

They are *so* upset.

In the owl vs. logger story, the loggers have stronger claim to our sympathies but do not quite succeed in totally convincing us that saving the remaining forest means extinction for them. Not being entirely convincing is now also the form. Even in the instance of the Mount St. Helens eruption, it is as odd to think that the mountain killed people accidently, as it would be to think the mountain did it purposefully. Accidental to what, naturally or deliberately killing animals? Incidental to providing us with an amazing spectacle?

Convincing is not what television is about. We are willing to settle for plausibility. It has all gotten very sophisticated, but not because it needs to be more sophisticated in order to deceive us. Little of the artifice of the Yellowstone coverage, and similarly confected news-constructs, escapes us. It has had to get sophisticated in order to entertain us. The Yellowstone Fires of 1988 was a public entertainment and a disaster to almost no one—not even to the careers of the pilloried public officials. All of us have perforce acquired fairly sophisticated interpretive skills. We note that reporters usually gets to tell the story they think is the right one. Television is too expensive for its owners to have reporters sent out wandering around *looking* for stories, they have to arrive on site with the story in hand. What they look for is setting and people to speak the lines. The person we see has made it on camera because they have stayed within the limits of the script. We know that. What we hope for is a break-out. We have acquired the art of staying afloat in the confluence of the reporter's story and that of the interviewee. We sense the tension between what the subject wants to say and what the reporter's question is framed to make he or she say. We then get both, what the reporter wants him to say and what he wants to say.

Learning to be sophisticated in this way is fun. Ducking what "they" are trying to foist on us is fun. Life is a movie, or a book, or a movie made from a book and we its urbane critics. We have the small, slightly mean, pleasure of the cynic. Making sense out of television, radio and print largely means not being taken in. Something about my talk with Robert made me want to give up my advantage as critic and find a role in the script. If there is a disaster, am I involved in any way other than as a spectator of the entertainment? I would have to read my experience into the story, to somehow get taken in.

From the East

A month later, June, I traveled back East to where I came west from, northwestern Connecticut. I did not go directly home but flew first to New York to stop with my brother on Long Island. I traveled to Boston from New York by train with a retired professor, J. Bruce Crabtree. We visited another retired professor friend, my former mountaineering partner, Bill Buckingham, who was dying of AIDS. Crabtree went back to New York and I went from Boston by bus to Dover, New Hampshire to visit my brother there, by automobile with him across New Hampshire into Vermont and down the back roads of western Massachusetts to Norfolk, where the other two of we five brothers live. We moved so often during the depression and first year of World War II that each of us was born in a different town. Norfolk, where the youngest was born, is the only town we all ever lived in together. My Long Island brother joined us the following day and we met to decide whether or not to put my mother in a home. As it turned out, this was the last time I was to see both Buckingham and my mother. Buckingham died six weeks later and my mother the following summer.

The first leg of this encirclement of the Northeast began slowly. Our train ran out of power just as we reached the north shore of Manhattan Island. Overlooking the complex waters at the confluence of the Harlem and East Rivers, hard by Randalls Island Park, it was a good place to break down. There was surprisingly little water traffic there compared to similarly out-of-the-main-harbor backwaters and side channels in Puget Sound or on the Columbia River. Possibly the fishing luck is not good there. While we sat watching a 14 foot runabout make its way downstream, followed a half-mile back by an 18 foot skiff, their wakes crossed by a tug, we were entertained by the trainmaster announcing over the public address system the progress of his thoughts about what might happen next.

Someone will be coming out soon to repair the electrics.

No, another engine would be coming from the city.

Uh, the other engine that will be coming will be coming down from New Haven.

Actually, what we think will be best is for you to get on the next train scheduled out of the station.

Watch your step as you climb down out of this train and cross the tracks to the other train.

We experienced further delays up the line, as they say. Passenger traffic is not the highest priority. The upshot was that all three trains scheduled out of New York that morning came into Boston the same time that evening, nose to tail, none of them on time. New England appeared to be prospering, Boston appeared to be thriving, but it means something that we cannot run a railroad the short distance between the most important city in the world and the most important city in New England.

Although my purpose was not to contemplate the future of the last 8% of what we used to call virgin forest, I could not avoid thinking about ways in which the East's past serves as a pattern for the West's future—at large and in my family. Most of us don't doubt that the graph of our nation's weal is a demurely declining line. We accept decline abstractly, many of us don't experience it in any striking way. My position as a college professor has declined at a rate of about one percent a year for the past twenty-five years. This is not a real decline; it is the decline within an abstraction, "professional position." My actual experience has been of slowly rising salary, rising equity in my home, rising respect and so forth. It is not until we have an actual reversal that we feel the giddy pull of the downward slope, feeling the ease of descent as compared to the solid work and worth of ascent. When you are struggling up a decline what you experience is an illusion of increasing weight and slow progress.

The beginning of my swing through New England was emblematic of decline; it felt as if the slope itself was slipping.

A Home in the Woods

Maine lost whatever chance it had to thrive years before my mother and father were born. Maine was cut over, as we say in the West, its virgin forests exported and replaced with puny trees. Its salmon runs were destroyed, its coastal fisheries depleted, and then the state was all but abandoned. The forests might grow back again, or not, apparently nobody much cared. Trees did grow back. When I lived there as a young child, no one ever told me what had happened, that there were once giant trees where now there were little spindly ones, so I did not know that they were spindly. Maine people were poor and always had been. In Maine, only poverty has proven to be sustainable. In spite of the monetary value of the vast forests that disappeared from the state, we had to import millionaires from out of state with which to salt the population of Bar Harbor.

My father's father was a blacksmith, in Ellsworth, Bar Harbor's neighbor. In the early years of the century, he was not able to earn a living in Maine shoeing horses and doing household and farm iron work, so he did iron work in the West, living for months in construction camps, making railroad bridges for logging and mining operations. At one point he seems to have had dreams of building up a big enough stake to move his family west. There are photographs from the one season he took his wife and son west with him out to Minnesota. He never got far enough west or far enough ahead to escape Maine. Those who did escape Maine later had to escape Minnesota, when the forests of the old Northwest were exhausted. They came to this coast, the second Northwest. Weyerhauser made that move from Minnesota, but won't be moving again, for the same reason that I won't be moving again, there is nowhere else to go. True, there is Alaska the final Northwest, but now we know that the last old growth tree outside of a park or wilderness area will be cut, the woodsman unsparing of that tree has to think about where he wants his family to end up. We have to pick the clear-cuts we want to settle down next to. My grandfather, by choice or necessity, lived out his life close to the logged forests of his youth, when they still did selective cutting. He was the last of our branch of the Sinclair clan to stay in Maine. The clear-cuts in Alaska seem exceptionally ugly in comparison to the astonishing wild majesty of the country. Not many are now, or are likely to be, interested in living by Alaskan clear-cuts. We are done pushing back the forest.

Fathers have been a luxury in our family, but not because of divorce. They went to war as did my father when I was six, or they went out West to find work, as his father had done when he was five, or they died of tuberculosis, as did my mother's father when she was six. He, Grandfather Coffin, entered history, if not heaven, leaving his wife, four sons, and two daughters to subsist on a 100-acre farm in Gray, Maine, the farm to which he retired when he was too sick to continue at the family shoe factory in Freeport. I have seen the farm three times and now share ownership of it.

Most of it is third growth Maine woods, pretty scruffy stuff. It was cleared the first time to make a farm some unrecorded time before my grandfather bought it. After her children grew up, my grandmother remarried, stopped farming and deeded the land to her second husband for his lifetime. He logged the second growth to, as the expression went, "pay for his old age" as if old age was a sin. I don't think the poor tired old farm will make a third growth in anything less than a half a millennium. There is one lovely open glen of about 10 acres. There are no trees on it because it is 10 acres of glacier-polished granite covered by one and three-quarters inches of soil and six inches of moss. In time, the farm could become prime real estate. It is now less than ten miles north of the perimeter of the continuous East Coast megalopolis. It seems not a good sign that this place that cannot naturally support a family could become prime real estate. On the other hand cities should be built on worthless land.

The farm as it was could support a family of widow and five children, but not six. Maine is nearly as cold as Alaska (much colder than Southeast Alaska) with none of the salmon runs, marine mammals, or caribou herds that makes subsistence living in Alaska a reasonable romantic fantasy. Life for my aunt, uncles and grandmother was subsistence living at the bottom of the higher primate food chain. The four older boys worked the farm and my grandmother ran the house and garden—the girls were supernumerary. My mother's sister was the baby, so she stayed. Mother went to live with her schoolteacher maiden aunt.

Auntie was a strong, intelligent woman, and attractive in the manner of Athena rather than Aphrodite. She and my mother returned to the farm every summer. Auntie restored Yankee spirit and discipline where her sister-in-law, who was a LaPierre, had allowed too much Mediterranean slack. From the point of view of their little sisters as well as their aunt, the brothers were just barely domesticated. Nevertheless, by this diligent two steps forward in the summer one step back in the winter renewal of civility and discipline, Auntie eventually prevailed. The brothers helped Russ get through Bowdoin and Harvard Law School. Si, Ernie, and Ray, with the help of Russ and each other, all went to medical school. Then they all went their own ways. None of them got rich, but they lived down the indignity of having to wear home-tailored trousers to high school. My uncles hated the farm as both symbol and instrument of the family's decline. They thought my mother fortunate to be off of it.

One way to look at my mother's young life is to think of her as having gone away to a private school with one teacher and one student. That is how my uncles thought of it. Nobody, including my mother herself, ever concerned themselves to ask her how she felt about being exiled from her family at age six. It is, however, in the nature of things that our loudest actions bespeak our loudest thoughts.

From the time I was born until my brother Bob, the fourth son, entered high school, my mother almost never left her house. She had to do the shopping while my father did WWII. She and my father played cards once a week with the neighbor across the driveway, but in the nineteen years I was at home, I can recall them going to dinner at the homes of friends but three times. Never to a movie, never to a restaurant, never to gossip, not even regularly to church did she go until the oldest four of us were out of her care. She went to our ceremonies at church and school, and she watched me run in a track meet once. She wouldn't go to another one because she found my custom of vomiting after running the mile unseemly. I've made her out to sound like just another one of those reclusive Yankees, but she was not. When my youngest brother went to school my mother got a job at the curculation desk in the library and loved being conversant with every literate person in town. In an exploited and broken country, an unbroken family is rare. While we were her responsibility, she enjoyed to the full the privilege of bringing us up.

The moral of this story, as I see it, is that we are adaptable and tough enough. Nevertheless, having to fight and connive in the effort to carry off something as basic as bringing the next generation along, though not rare in post-industrial history, is not an indication of a thriving people. If you're not right with your place, it is exceedingly difficult to be right with each other as a family, as a community, as a people. The owl is not the enemy of families. Whether because of greed or honest miscalculation, sustainable yield has turned out to be a fond wish at best, at worst a cynical ruse to deceive those who don't live here and to placate we rubes who do. What loggers believed to be a form of farming a renewable crop, clear cut logging, resembles dredging gold more than mowing hay. As with farming and mining, logging has become increasingly capital intensive. We have seen this pattern not once but repeatedly. Each time we seem not to have known what we were doing, what we had done, nor did we or do we have in mind a probable future.

Knowledge and Experience

In the same way 19th Century British officers and gentleman carried their tea service into the bush, we New Englanders include in our kit a list of self-imposed responsibilities. Knowing the fate of the last of our ancient forests had inserted itself onto my list. Knowing means . . . well it's hard to say. It does not just mean making a prophecy; predicting the end of the world is a very much overrated skill. Nor does knowing equate with information. Information is not knowledge as owning a place is not belonging there. Respectable, certifiable knowing: philosophy, the law, or diesel mechanics, tends to require the permission of your department. As a literature professor I have permission to examine "art" stories, stories of unpopular culture and, if I get to feeling lonely and out of touch, and don't wander into the kingdoms of the social scientists, I am allowed to comment on stories of popular culture in an undisciplined way. As for politics, in my department only Marxists, feminists, or Post-modernists are allowed to utter that word unsarcastically. I am only Marxist and feminist, when I'm reading something by one. I don't plan to become post-modernist until I'm dead. I've already presented my non-qualifications as natural scientist or natural historian. Earning the right to know things is as problematic as earning a right to a place.

There are two common ways to get around departmental ownership of knowledge. One way is to become a preacher. As a preacher you assert whatever God moves you to assert, which is seldom departmentalized—in spite of a number of efforts throughout history to persuade ourselves that God reads Aristotle. The other is to become a journalist and pretend to be asserting nothing. Journalists are permitted to make of themselves conduits to pass the high culture of the departments of physics, commerce, education, and athletics—as well as those of State, Justice, Defense, and Interior—down to the culture of the populace. The rub is, the first requires a devoted, and the second a large, audience.

Thanks to a devising of my philosopher colleague, Mark Levensky, I was in possession of a third means of swiping apples of knowledge from walled gardens. At Mark's suggestion, a group of faculty from various disciplines, interested in wilderness either professionally or personally, formed a wilderness study group. We are one each in English, philosophy, physics, geology, art, and filmmaking; plus we have four brands of biologist: ecology, entomology, marine biology, and bio-physics, the latter a recent president of the Sierra Club. Wilderness is my department. I may be a little short of certain qualifications but my pals have a bunch of qualifications and are willing to tell me anything I am capable of understanding. Making sure that you aren't going to be blindsided by the experts is one part of achieving understanding. Understanding is what you need if you don't have outright expertise, maybe even if you do.

The other necessity is appropriate experience. When you are there to not hear the soundless flight of an owl, you are in a position to achieve understanding. If, like Robert, you see for yourself, then you have an idea. You can do something with an idea. Seeing for yourself and getting an idea makes a good way to start. Take a little experience, toss it into a private think tank, things begin to bubble.

The "Wilderness Department" offered two courses. In the spring term of 1990, the term we were in when I went down to Oregon to see the spotted owl, Mark Levensky and I team-taught "Seeing What's There." This was, as a colleague pointed out to me, possibly the first field program in the humanities since the Canterbury pilgrimage. The complete title was "Seeing What's There: Washington Landscapes." The landscapes we saw were: estuary, delta, ocean beach, bay, forest, river, basin, sand dune, lake, desert pothole country, rain forest, city, and volcano. We missed seeing the islands of Puget Sound, the Strait of Juan de Fuca, an alpine landscape, pine and juniper forest, desert plateau, or the vast wheat fields of far eastern Washington.

Our first three-day field trip in "Seeing What's There" was to the ocean. There two students wearing heavy packs nearly drowned by getting themselves plucked off a jutting point by a wave. The last field-trip of the quarter was a one-day climb of Mt. St. Helens. There a student fell out of her footsteps in the snow while standing still. Her slide was stopped by two guys wearing conventional skis and a guy on a snow board, but she thought it was all over. We lost students for period of from one to six hours on five out of the seven other field trips. These difficulties in knowing where we were competed with the assigned work as the major content of the course. We spent almost as much time looking for students who weren't there as we did seeing what was there. As might be expected of students who would go to a college offering such courses, a sizable minority of the students in the course thought that their disorientation was attributable to the character of their two faculty. I began to believe them.

So it came to pass that in the fall of 1990 I was teaching an intensive course called "Wilderness and Temporality." The title was contrived to sound serious enough that if nothing else interesting developed, we could try to figure out what the title meant. Titles with abstract nouns, like "Wilderness and Temporality," help put off students who see a field program as an opportunity to get credit for going camping.

The appeal of being with students in the field having somewhat diminished for me by the time of this second course, I met with them for a week to firm-up their projects and then sent them off alone on two-week field trips of their own design. Fears that students might want credit for camping turned out to be unfounded. One student went to the field, the other seventeen either went to the library or nowhere. I headed for Wrangell, Alaska.

One other reason for going to Alaska was that, according to an article published in the local paper in August, "Pacific Northwest loggers are increasingly looking in the vast rain forests of Southeast Alaska [for work] as the number of logging jobs decline with the shrinking timber supply in Washington and Oregon."[8] My reason for landing in Wrangell was that Wrangell was where John Muir landed in Alaska in 1879 after stopping in our area for "a few weeks":

> The most interesting of these [short excursions] and the most difficult to leave was the Puget Sound region, famous the world over for the wonderful forests of gigantic trees about its shores. It is an arm and many-fingered hand of the sea, reaching southward from the Straits of Juan de Fuca about a hundred miles into the head of one of the noblest coniferous forests on the face of the globe. All its scenery is wonderful—broad river-like reaches sweeping in beautiful curves around bays and capes and jutting promontories, opening here and there into smooth, blue, lake-like expanses dotted with islands and feathered with tall spiry evergreens, their beauty doubled on the bright mirror-water.

and:

> On the way up to Olympia, then a hopeful little town situated at the end of one of the longest fingers of the Sound, one is often reminded of Lake Tahoe, the scenery of the

8. "Northwest loggers look north for work," 8/12/1990, The Olympian, 8/12/1990, sec. E.

widest expanses is so lake-like in the clearness and still-
ness of the water and the luxuriance of the surrounding
forests. Doubling cape after cape, passing uncounted islands, new combinations break on the view in endless variety, sufficient to satisfy the lover of wild beauty through
a whole life.

"The lover of wild beauty" will find here still "broad river-like
reaches sweeping in beautiful curves" but the water is not so clear
nor the trees as spiry. As for the magnificent Douglas Fir "specimen I
measured near Olympia [that] was about three hundred feet in height
and twelve feet in diameter four feet above the ground," one hopes
that it at least left Puget Sound as the timbers and planking of an
almost equally magnificent sailing vessel.

On the other hand, the lover of wild beauty who follows Muir to
Alaska (and doesn't peer too intently) may still see what Muir saw,
nearly as he saw it:

> To the lover of pure wildness Alaska is one of the most
> wonderful countries in the world. No excursion that I know
> of may be made into any other American wilderness where
> so marvelous an abundance of mobile, newborn scenery
> is so charmingly brought to view as on the trip through-
> out the Alexander Archipelago to Fort Wrangell and Sitka.

Other than that, my intentions in going to Wrangell were nebu-
lous. I was perilously close to going in order to experience experience. Not knowing what I was looking for, I thought to find it on
Prince Of Wales Island, where most of the logging in Alaska had been
done and was still being done. To do that, I didn't really have to go to
Wrangell, which isn't even on Prince of Wales Island. The easiest way
to get to POW, as it is called, was by ferry to the town of Hollis. Fact
is I didn't want to go to Hollis, I wanted to go to Coffman Cove.
Wrangell is closer to Coffman Cove than is Hollis. The disadvantage
was that to get to Coffman Cove from Wrangell I would have to cross
Clarence Strait. Since I didn't have a good reason for going to POW,
I didn't have a good reason not to go to Wrangell.

I met a logger from Coffman Cove two years before, in December 1988, two months after the Yellowstone Fires of '88.

By the time the afternoon flight from Sitka landed in Ketchikan, the dozen young bachelor loggers, who were waiting to fly "outside" for the winter closing of logging in Southeast, had taken advantage of a couple of extra hours of drinking time. They were in a festive mood when they came on board, talking loud and semi-tough, pulling cans of beer out of their pockets.

"I thought we were going to have to clean out that airport, didn't you Jim?"

"Yeah, we still might have to clean out this airplane if they didn't save us enough seats."

"Naw, I think I'll just sit on this pretty lady's lap. Or would you rather sit on mine? "

The stewardesses laughingly worked the aisles, loading baggage into the overhead lockers, ignoring the contraband beer cans. My seat was on the aisle. Predictably, the largest of the two loggers sat in the middle seat beside me. He was Scandinavian, both Norwegian and Swedish is my guess, with hair the color of fog-bleached straw. There was plenty of room in his seat for his hips but too little backrest for his shoulders. I'm six feet tall with my shoes on, which they were, and he talked to his buddies ahead, behind, and across the aisle without having to peer around my or anybody else's head. He was the leader of this crew, at least the party leader. The other guys turned towards him even as they spoke to someone else.

I had open to the first page *The Untamed Garden: and Other Personal Essays*, by David Raines Wallace.

"That looks like a good book, is it? I was reading that there," he said, pointing toward the middle of the page. I looked down at, "The ground I was trifling with wasn't my property, so not having to make mortgage payments on it, I was spared the more depressing implications of my incompetence."

We talked for the two hours into Seattle. He spotted me as a teacher right away, and gave me to know that he was a respecter of teachers as well as well-written books. I in turn let him know that I knew that his craft was a dangerous one—he was a cutter—and I hoped he could avoid injury. He told me that he happened to be a fast worker but not because he ever allowed himself to be hurried. He had been doing it for a long time, he was twenty-eight and had made cutter by the time he finished high school. If he had a regret, and he wasn't sure that he did, it would be that he hadn't pursued a career in music.

He had befriended the daughter of the principal of the High School in Coffman Cove, and was helping her with her guitar playing. It was unusual for a girl to play guitar, she was good, and he wanted to encourage her to get out of Coffman Cove and stick with her music. "Don't get me wrong, there's no...she's only 17 and I would never...you know, take advantage..." and he said no more but continued to shake his head determinedly, no, certainly not, no way, no. I believed absolutely that he wouldn't take advantage of her, so obviously in love with her was he. Maybe I'd hear some music in Coffman Cove.

For a while, it seemed as if I might have as much difficulty leaving Puget Sound as Muir had. As I would be alone, and using a sea-kayak to cross Clarence strait, I was considerable edgy about going to Southeast Alaska as late in the year as October. To allay one source of nervousness, I called the Alaska Marine Highway office in Juneau Friday morning, to ask, "Is the *Matanuska* leaving Bellingham this evening at 1830 as scheduled?" and got another lesson in leaving well enough alone. A colleague of mine says, "Everyone worries to their maximum capability." That's a maxim I have no difficulty believing and remembering, but I always overlook its implication that if you remove one worry it will of necessity be replaced by another.

"*Yes*," she said cheerily. "Didn't I just talk to you? Did you just call?"

"No, I haven't called you for a year. I'm calling from Olympia."

"Actually it's the *Columbia*, not the *Matanuska*. I thought you were the man who just called. He was listening to our weather. Winds of 75 miles per hour are predicted."

"*They are*! Good Lord."

"They won't be here when you get here," she said laughing at my alarm, or my quaint expletive. It was quite the thrill I got as I pictured myself crossing Clarence Strait in my kayak and being hit with such a wind.

That was the first of the signs that this passage was not going to be smooth sailing. As I approached Seattle on the drive up to the ferry, an hour out of Olympia, I realized that I had left my paddle behind. This, I knew, was not everyday professorial brain damage caused by attending faculty meetings, this was a trick my sub-conscious had picked up in my mountaineering days. When I was committed to doing a climb that made me more than usually tense, I would leave a piece of equipment behind—not something serious enough to abort the climb, just a little excuse for what might prove to be a less than brilliant performance on my part. Thus, in setting out to do the second complete ascent of the South Buttress of Mount Moran with Jake Breitenbach, Bill Buckingham, and Barry Corbet, my first climb using direct aid, I left one of the two stirrups I needed behind. I understand that my sub-conscious is in this way doing its best to help me out, but my sub-conscious is a very poorly calibrated instrument. While substituting a stupid worry for the appropriate one, it usually manages to make things harder as well. I managed the climb with one stirrup, at one point standing on my thumb for a foothold.

A replacement paddle would cost $150. I had left in time to arrive at the ferry in plenty of time, but not time enough to lengthen the trip by 120 with an extra Seattle to Olympia round trip. I had a choice of trying to find a rental paddle in Seattle, or changing my destination from Wrangell to Juneau or Sitka where there are kayaking equipment rental places. At the third shop I tried in Seattle, I was able to rent a paddle for three weeks for the two-week rate. I got the break because the paddle was scheduled to be included in a sale the next day where I would have been able to buy it for about what I was renting it for. Now I could worry about money. One could always worry about money; that's one of money's chief values.

My daughter dropped me off in time. There were only 250 passengers on this trip, about a third of the number of passengers there would have been on board in the summer, so I had no difficulty finding a prime spot on the deck and under the solarium to sleep. Things to worry about were disappearing at an alarming rate.

Thirty minutes before departure, the purser announced that we were now on Alaska time. Technically, we were already in Alaska.

We departed as scheduled on Pacific Daylight Time and so got to spend that hour a second time, watching Pacific daylight departing westward, the dark that spread slowly from the east pushing the pink down over the horizon. In the bar I purchased the last Alaskan beer, the pale not the amber I preferred, but I was glad to have it. I had a long, hot shower, then a roast beef dinner in the uncrowded dining room. Finally I relaxed. I laughed at my leaving the paddle behind, picturing it as I last saw it beside my work bench, near the sharpening stone. It doesn't do to take things out of their places. The paddle resides in the kayak. I took it out to get a measurement from it. I was making a paddle out of wood. Not like Nels, the anthropologist/nature writer, Richard K. Nelson, who makes his out of a two-by-four with just an axe and hunting knife, I was... "Hunting knife! Oh shit, beside the sharpening stone."

My mind is capable of remarkable feats of remembering as well as forgetting. I remembered nearly simultaneously both that I forgot my hunting knife and that there would be no stores open in Wrangell at the time we were scheduled to dock. It would be late Sunday afternoon when we arrived, and Wrangell takes little notice of the ferry's arrival. Nothing stays open to accommodate ferry passengers.

The ferry arrived at Wrangell at 6 p.m., less than an hour to dark, a 15 knot wind blowing rain from the south. I unloaded my kayak and went looking for a hunting knife. I found a Swiss Army knife in the drugstore. About twenty minutes to go to dark. As best as I had been able to tell by studying the shore from the deck as we had approached, it was ten miles from the landing to a suitable camping place, three hours paddling if the current wasn't against me.

Most Southeast Alaska towns are built on a narrow shelf of land between the water and a mountainside. Really every town except Petersburg has this on-a-shelf form. Petersburg is on an island peninsula whose mountains got clipped by the last glacier that came through. Southeast towns are a few blocks deep "downtown," (two blocks in Wrangell, ten in Juneau) and 12 to 20 miles long, one road deep along the shore, stretched out both ways from the center. At least in Wrangell the ferry terminal is downtown. In Sitka and Juneau the terminals are, respectively 7 and 12 miles from town. Nature has done her best to suggest that the Alexander Archipelago is not prime real estate for urban development.

When Muir came to Wrangell, he was headed up onto the mountain behind the town to camp when a missionary offered him lodging in the mission carpenter shop. Because of my kayak, I needed to be near the water and couldn't go up on the mountainside. When the *Columbia* set sail from Bellingham two days earlier, winds in northern Clarence Strait were 84 knots. What I was experiencing was markedly improved from that. Somehow that failed to comfort me. I looked back down Zamovia Strait at the large dark cloud rolling up the strait between the mountains. I turned on my little weather radio: thirty knots tomorrow, forty knots Tuesday. A room for three days would be 210 dollars. I went back into the terminal, bought a ticket for Sitka, where there are friends who would take me in, and hauled my kayak back on board.

One small advantage of age is that after you have had the same experience about a hundred times it begins to feel familiar. The advantage would be huge if the feeling came before the fact, where feeling this has happened before might do you some good. Unfortunately, only prophets and shaman remember the future. To have been scared under the circumstances prevailing as I bounced off and on the ferry was reasonable. Fight or flight. Not well equipped by experience or skill to fight, so flight. I came to Wrangell planning to kayak to Coffman Cove; there was too much wind (or there might be), I changed my plans.

A reasonable account but not a true one. Sly fear. Lovely fear. I knew too well not to trust fear that comes when there is no immediate or inevitable danger. I knew as soon as the *Columbia* pulled away from the ferry dock in Wrangell that I was not fleeing shipwreck in Clarence Strait. Fear, I have long known, has many uses. It is always real and that can be a comfort when its causes are better left unseen: when, for example, you need to escape from a situation where you don't know what you are doing, or do know, but are afraid it's not the right thing to be doing. As I reclaimed my steamer chair, I pondered why, in my impulsive decision to return to the ferry, had I given not one thought to back-up plans for rough weather; the plan to take advantage of the fact that Wrangell is where John Muir landed in Alaska, for example? My business was not in Wrangell, why I didn't yet quite know—but I felt greatly relieved to be headed further north. What about my logger? It became suddenly clear to me that I did not need to know how it came out with the logger and the principal's daughter, nor did I have to struggle through ugly clear-cuts in the wind and rain in order to report the unpleasantness of it. I was startled to discover that what I had been saying all along, that loggers are not the problem, is true. I didn't need more intimate knowledge of what I already knew.

A cup of coffee in hand, I joined Phil Moreno, a Tlingit carver who was also headed for Sitka. As he had been since we left Bellingham, he was making jewelry at a table in the cafeteria. We teamed up for the rest of the passage. Phil's father was a fisherman from Mexico who worked his way through fished-out waters up the coast until he found Alaska and Phil's Tlingit mother. Both parents died when Phil was young. He and his brother were raised by the Catholic school in Skagway, a school that earned Phil's gratitude. When the ferry stopped in Skagway, we climbed up to a lake on the mountainside above town that Phil used to visit when he was in school. He hadn't been there in 40 years and it released an anthology of memories for him.

Later on the passage, outbound from Juneau to Sitka, in the course of chatting about people I knew or had met in Sitka, I mentioned the name of an active, and effective, conservationist to whom I had been introduced.

"Yeah, I know him," said Phil, "I hate that little bastard. Because of him we were split. He had us fighting each other." I didn't pursue the matter but assumed he was talking about either or both the decision his people made not to log Admiralty Island or the decision they made *to* log off their lands on Chichigoff Island.

A year earlier, in those very same waters, the confluence of Lynn Canal, Icy Strait and Chatham Strait, I met another Tlingit. It was sunny and 71° in Juneau on Friday 8th of September 1989, the record high for that day and the record latest day of the year to be as warm. It wasn't quite that warm at the ferry landing on Auke Bay 12 miles north of town, or on the deck of the little *Le Conte*, one of the two smaller vessels in the Southeast Alaska Marine Highway System, but it was warm enough so that all the chairs were full and people were lounging on the steel plate of the afterdeck. The *Le Conte* services the Tlingit communities of Hoonah, Angoon, and Kake, and the small villages of Pelican and Tenakee, little places tucked away in little bays and coves along the waters between the larger towns of Skagway, Haines, Juneau, Sitka, and Petersburg. At least half the passengers on board were Tlingit. I overheard a person say that about 40 of the Tlingit were returning to their villages from a large funeral in Town, as Juneau is termed by the folks living along Chatham and Icy Straits, as in, "I'm spending the winter in Town." Before the boat got underway, mindful of what a declining sun and the 18 knot breeze created by the vessel's own way would do to the comfort factor out there, I gave up my chair in the sun to a woman more grateful than she would have been had she known my motive and went forward to the Observation Lounge and found a chair in the front row.

In the seat next to me was Thomas Jack, a Tlingit, retired now from fishing, which he had done for fifty-five straight of his seventy-nine years. Thomas was deaf and was seated to my right, my bad ear side, but in spite of the fact that he could hear nothing I said, and I missed a certain amount of what he said, we chatted away happily all the way to Hoonah, where he lived and I was disembarking with my kayak to proceed westward along Icy Strait. People with hearing problems listen not at all or they listen very intently, which compensates more than a little for their dated receiving equipment.

Thomas Jack—still owns his seiner, prefers Cats to Gimmies in diesels—explained to me how the ferry skipper should have rounded Couverden Island at the end of the peninsula that divides the Lynn Canal from Icy Strait. It is quite a sight there at the confluence of Lynn Canal, leading north to Skagway; Icy Strait, reaching west out past Glacier Bay to the Gulf of Alaska; and Chatham Strait, running south from Skagway over two-hundred nautical miles through the northern two-thirds of the Alexander Archipelago to enter the Northeast Pacific. Above these then calm but current beswirled waters the stark summits and glaciers of the Fairweather Range, the St. Elias

Mountains, and the Coast Range softened as the setting sun pulled out from their glittering white snows shades of pink and blue and hues in between of which only painters know the names. All that was displayed above was reflected on and in the water in deeper and darker hues. In that light, choosing your view with care, you could manage not to see any clear-cuts.

Thomas called my attention to Mt. Fairweather of the ironic name, whose delicately sculpted beauty is rarely seen. That mountain was theirs, he told me, and always had been, always. That settled, he proceeded to the task of acquainting me with the dangers of navigating in Icy Strait without insulting me by implying that I lacked the necessary seamanship, sense, or, if it came to that, courage. Although he was old enough to be my father, I too was a grandfather. If someone with gray in his beard decides to paddle around up there in a kayak, you have to assume that something got him that far: if not common sense, dumb luck is okay too. I let him know that in hearing about South Inian Pass I had developed considerable respect for it. In the manner of courtesy between seamen, Thomas Jack refrained from issuing a small craft warning but told a story about being caught in South Inian Pass with the ebb opposed to wind waves, building an unusually heavy ocean surge. It was a very short story told mainly with the hands. The hands are held flat, palms down, one hand behind the other, and then are tilted up, the lower hand directly in front of the face, fingertips touching the heel of the other above. "Like this!" he said, snapping his hands into position, then adjusting his lower hand, representing his 48' seiner, to an angle just off the vertical—no need to exaggerate—and adjusting the upper to almost nothing off the vertical, representing the green wave curling above his pilot house window; he getting through the breaking crest just before the whole wave becomes a comber. Then there is a powerful sucking of air into the chest, the way you do to cram your stomach back down where it belongs when it rises up. Once again, "Like this," the hands pointed up, less of a snap this time, more reflectively positioned to the proper angle, then a laugh. I laughed too, less heartily, as is appropriate when you are not in the relaxed, amused position of having been afraid and lived to tell it, but in the other position, the position of anticipating what's coming to you. With that expressive device established in our vocabulary, we turned to other matters but came back to stories using the boat hand and the wave hand twice more in our four hours of talking.

Thomas gave me detailed instructions about how to approach Gustavus, the town near the entrance of Glacier Bay, the primary destination of kayakers in Southeast, in case I went there, and Elfin Cove, which is on the ocean side of South Inian Pass. There, he said, they would tell me when it would be good to head across the stretch of open coast toward Pelican. The implication was that this would be a more serious enterprise than the others. (In the event, I took that hint and did not attempt the passage to Pelican.) The conversation with Thomas Jack was largely one-way not only because he could speak more fluently than I could write on his little pad, but because we both knew that I needed what he knew more than he needed what I knew, or had experienced. Many people on the boat, white and native, seemed to know him and all nodded or spoke to him with familiar but obviously respectful gestures and tones. I would have known he was an elder, a man to whom it is a privilege to listen, even without these signs.

We could assume as seamen that from this that we had in common came our most interesting experiences of the world. Thomas showed no interest in knowing why I was there; it was plausible that a person might want to be there in order to be there. He wondered where I was going to sleep in Hoonah. I made a tent with my hands. "Well," he said, "I guess you'll get acquainted. I'll show you the restaurant. Maybe somebody will let you put your tent in their yard."

There was one moment when I thought that Thomas Jack may have wanted something from me. As we approached the northeast shore of Chichagof Island, about where we began seeing the clear-cuts, he talked about the logging. "Seven hundred miles of road they've built out from Hoonah, all up through the hills...and millions, millions, I don't know, maybe billions of board feet sent to Japan from right there." He watched my face as he spoke which he had not done before, as if to see what I thought. He went on, "The young guys like it, they make twenty-two dollars an hour right away, in maybe a year. When they get out of high school, before even, in the summer, they can get a job and make twenty-two dollars an hour." Rounding *Pt. Sophia*, nothing in my face, he continued, "Have you seen this new logging with the tower?" I shook my head no, which was not exactly true. I had seen logging with the tower but I hadn't seen the *old* type of logging for comparison. I had no basis for comment. "It's pretty fast," he said, showing with his hands the lead line cable hauling a log up a slope. Then after a pause, "It's *really* fast." I nodded. I wasn't meaning to be coy or unresponsive with my views; I didn't know what they were. I wasn't even certain that what sounded to me to be a conversational lead really was one.

The *Le Conte* slowed at that point, the point inside Pt. Sophia that sheltered Hoonah from winds from the northeastern quadrant, and our conversation ended there. Across the entrance to Port Frederick there was a log ship exactly like those that carried logs from the Port of Olympia to Japan.

The ferry car deck was so crowded with cars and baggage that it took almost two hours for the ferry to get cargo and passengers off-loaded. Instead of going to town, I unrolled my sleeping bag beside my kayak under the back eave of the ferry terminal for the night. I left on the morning ebb and eventually paddled beyond the sights and sounds of clear-cut logging. Before I left that morning, I walked through the graveyard across the road from the ferry landing. There was a marker there for a woman who lived to be 115 years old. What had she thought about what was happening to the forest that was theirs, the Tlingit's, even more surely than Mt. Fairweather was theirs? That would have been my question for Thomas Jack. I did not ask it because I sensed that he did not know what he thought about what was happening to his forest, that he had been speaking to me in the way we have of telling a person what we have seen in hopes that in the telling we may ourselves see what befell us. Or maybe he just had to say it to himself, to see if he could hear if he understood it.

I didn't really know how Thomas Jack thought about selling their forest, nor do I know what Phil Mareno thought about timbering on Tlingit land. What he was talking to me about was whites. How I

understand what he said is that the whites had taken an entire conti-
nent from the natives, and except for a few national parks, exploited
it entirely: animal, vegetable, mineral, its very soil. Now, by some
quirk of history, we were prevented from doing the same with a few
thousand acres of Pacific Rainforest that belonged to his people. Our
advice to the natives is not to do as we have done. "You'll exhaust
your resource base. Your children will never forgive you." What Phil
sees is that "they"—intelligent, well-educated, multi-advantaged
whites, who make up the cadre of environmentalists—pretend not to
know that the only resource that matters, that works, the only resource that is truly renewable in this culture, is money, capital. We
side with natives who decide to try to regain their traditional culture,
and look with sorrow on those poor souls who are doing precisely as
we have done. Meanwhile, the children of environmentalists will take
their places in the privileged classes of the dominant culture, or not,
as they please; they have a choice. Tlingit children will have no such
option. With capital they may have a chance to survive as a people
and save a portion of their culture. Without it, many will survive as
individuals, more or less well depending on arbitrary and unpredictable circumstances, but the Tlingit people will disappear. Phil does
not appear to believe that environmentalists act as they do because of
a racist conspiracy. He said, "They just do not understand that we
have to have *something* to develop in order to survive." He means, I
think, precisely that we don't understand; we don't get it. If racism is
involved it lies in our proceeding as if we knew that we aren't required to understand.

Whether Phil really means "hate," with reference to the environmental activist, I don't know. I suspect that he might mean "contempt." From Phil's point of view, again as I see it, failure to understand the position of the people you are telling how to live is a form
of contempt and requires contempt in return.

A Press of One's Own
Speaking for Loggers

On that same 1989 trip as my talk with Thomas Jack, in the gift shop of the ferry, I discovered a book about logging in Alaska in which hatred and conspiracy are important themes. I noticed the book because its title was also the title of my research project, "People of the Tongass." The subtitle, "Alaska Forestry Under Attack," I misread as Alaska *forests* under attack. Reading further put me right: "Introduction by the Alaska Congressional Delegation: Senator Ted Stevens, Senator Frank H. Murkowski and Representative Don Young," and published by The Free Enterprise Press, a division of the Center for the Defense of Free Enterprise.

In their opening lines, the authors, K. D. Soderberg and Jackie DuRette, make no pretext of objectivity:

> An ounce of truth to cure a ton of lies.
>
> That's what this book is and why we wrote it.
>
> We have done our best to provide here a necessary antidote to the massive dose of media poison presently being penned against the resource users of the Tongass National Forest. This book is the outraged response by two Alaskans to an unscrupulous campaign of environmentalist slander being waged by media ranging from the respected *Life, Reader's Digest, The New Republic,* and *Sports Illustrated,* to tourist periodicals including *Conde Nast's Traveler, Alaska Magazine,* and *Trailer Life,* to publications clearly having a special-interest axe to grind such as *Sierra, Audubon,* and *Backpacker.*[9]

and:

> "To mix my own metaphor of fair warning, if 'environmentalism' is a sacred cow to you, prepare to have your ox gored."[10]

The "unscrupulous campaign of environmentalist slander" is a conspiracy by journalists and environmentalists to convince the world that logging destroys the forest. That logging destroys the forest, we are given to know, is a proposition so absurd that the conspirators could only pitch it to us because few of us have direct knowledge of logging and we are innocent of the boundless perfidy of the conspirators. Hence the need for their side of the story. The weapon with which Soderberg and DuRette propose to do their goring is an article in the March 14, 1988 *Sports Illustrated* by Jack Scow, "one of the most dishonest 'Tongass Trashers" we've ever seen."[11] The first thrust is a chapter titled "Liars," which is a close reading of Scow's piece, "The Forest Service Follies." Perhaps his title is the source of the authors' penchant for alliteration:

> Punch, punch, punch, punch, punch. Whew! What a slugger! Jack Scow, the best virtuoso voice of venom, vituperation and viciousness we've ever heard. You have to admit that when he gets through, there's not much left.[12]
>
> Scow, they reveal, is a former college classmate of Steve Richardson of the Wilderness Society, who in turn is an old friend of Robert Mrasek, the leading House sponsor of bills to reform forest management on the Tongass. A journalist, a congressman and a big shot environmentalist, were they able to include a lawyer and a used car salesman, the bottom of the barrel of respectability would have been scraped clean. For the lawyer we must wait until Chapter Eight, "Proving Ground for Lawyers." It begins:
>
> Q: What's the difference between finding a dead lawyer and a dead skunk in the middle of the highway?
>
> A: There are skid marks in front of the skunk.

9. People of the Tongass, p.xiii.
10. People of the Tongass, 19.
11. People of the Tongass, 21.
12. People of the Tongass, 26.

There are no used car salesmen.

People of the Tongass is not an easy book to read. Their argument so entangled in rhetorical manipulation that it refutes itself by the skepticism aroused. For that and other reasons, it is all but impossible to figure out who they imagine to be their audience. Their argument is that environmentalist are both wrong and not nice people while loggers are homey people who heroically provide us wood for our homes. The conspiracy to destroy the economy of these plain good folks they see as having two motivations: the necessity to justify the high salaries of the executive directors of environmental groups and hatred of loggers. Who do they really expect to believe that Scow wrote his article to justify the high salary of Richardson and because he hates loggers? Loggers maybe? It's really hard to know. If we the unknowing are their audience, Soderberg and DuRette apparently want us to believe that not only is Skow is a liar involved in a conspiracy to make us hate loggers, he means to do with an article berating the forest service. Skow makes no mention of loggers in the *Sports Illustrated* piece. As its title suggests, "The Forest Service Follies," really is about the forest service; the authors' say as much later in their book.

If we are the audience, the fact that loggers are not in the article forces us to wonder wherein lies the hatred of loggers, in us?

They wants us to believe that Scow attacks loggers at least partly in order to help justify the high salary of one of his friends. This is hard to fathom no matter who is the subject of his article. If they truly believe that Scow's criticism of the forest service is an attack on loggers, why don't they explain why the attack is disguised as a critique of the forest service or how an attack on the forest service amounts to an attack on loggers? Suppose they are counting on most of their audience both not reading Skow's piece and not noticing that they tell us themselves that the piece is an attack on the Forest Service. What does that say about their stated purpose of countering the lies told to millions by these magazines with huge readerships?

How about this. People, even journalists, are no more inclined to blame loggers for logging than they are cowboys for overgrazing.

DuRette and Soderberg know that and in fact are counting on it—for something. Perhaps that's for them the strongest evidence that there is a conspiracy. They know that Scow knows that we aren't inclined to blame the loggers for overcutting. The fact that Skow doesn't mention loggers reveals that he knows that we aren't inclined to blame loggers; his not mentioning them is conclusive evidence of how deeply imbedded his hatred is of loggers. The slimy son-of-bitch doesn't even have the guts to say what his real motives are.

Okay. But if they are that sophisticated and perceptive, and believe that we are too, they are certainly sophisticated enough to realize that we are going to wonder about their economic motives.

There is something very odd about the tone resulting from the authors' handling of loggers in their own piece. Of the book's 350 pages, 265 are interviews of and testimonials by "people of the Tongass." Over 160 names are indexed. It gets more than a little folksy in there and we, readers of *Conde Nast's Traveler*, are not spared: "Well, did you get enough of breakfast, faithful reader? Don't forget to make a sack lunch for yourself. The fixin's are all laid out on the tables by the far wall. You can fill your steel Thermos with coffee over there in the corner."

Very few of those interviewed are actively what most people think of as a logger, a person working on a crew that cuts down trees. In chapter five, "Loggers," there is but one, Louie White, a Tlingit who got into logging in 1982, "My last year in high school. I was born in Hoonah in 1964 and I was going to be a senior in '82, and I needed money to go to college. Logging happened to show up about at that time." Louie logged for five years before falling 75 feet out of a tree.

> I had nightmares at first, waking up in the hospital. They put a full-length cast on me at first, and I'd wake up jerking really hard and kept snapping my bone, so they had to pin it. Two operations right in a row. I kept having nightmares about it. But there's something about logging that really gets to be part of you. I didn't go back to climbing for a while. But I'm climbing again. I've overcome my fear. This time I'm a lot more careful.

We are happy to learn that Louie and his wife are planning to go to college and come back to Hoonah as teachers. That section is called "Skyfall." It's followed by "The Turning Wheel of Terror," in which Louie's story reminds Jackie of an experience she had. Her husband Butch was up in the woods when a young employee of his was killed in an accident. Butch builds roads so we don't know if this industrial accident is an accident of a logger, just that it is an accident while logging. After we are told that of the 120 people up in the woods that day 118 came down, leaving Butch and the corpse up there alone until the MedEvac, no cancel that, coroner, state troopers and safety people, join him. Butch then "picked up our lifeless friend and put him gently, like a son, on a stretcher, put the stretcher in the back of a crummy [bus] and drove the crummy down the hill . . ." Butch stopped in front of the lad's house and sends someone down to fetch the lad's wife, so he can persuade her that she doesn't want to see the remains. She says she had to. He says that if she trusts him she won't, so of course she doesn't. The body is taken away and Butch comes home.

> Butch came back to camp. I kept out of his way. Our two boys were in the house and kept quiet. There wasn't a kid out playing anywhere. Butch had just been grilled by three layers of government, talked to a bereaved wife and put the body of a friend on a plane to cold storage in Juneau. He needed some breathing space.

But she didn't give him enough. She decides to make some lunch and wash Butch's clothes for him.

> I was just bending down to pick up his hickory shirt and shake it off when Butch came out of the bathroom . . . [and] grabbed the shirt away from me so hard I almost went flying. He said keep your goddam hands off that shirt. I don't want you or anybody ever touching these clothes. He grabbed everything off the floor, stormed outside to the burning barrel, threw the clothes in the burning barrel and set them all afire. . . . Late that afternoon he started talking to me. When we'd talked a while I said, tell me, Butch, tell me: why did you burn your clothes? He

looked at me and his eyes filled with tears. He said I did it because his brains were all over that shirt. I couldn't stand for anybody to ever see that.

Sensitive guy.

Sensitive authors: "You stay at this business long enough and someone will make a fatal move. . . . We'll never know if he was distracted by worry over an early season shutdown caused by some lawsuit or if he was coming down with the flu or what. He was gone. That's all." Think about that, you environmentalists, do you ever think about the effect you are going to have on the mood and alertness of loggers when you sue?

This is followed by the rhetorical highpoint of the book.

> Then when the Jack Skows and the Steve Richardsons and the Robert Mrazeks of the world come to destroy us we don't hate them. We despise them for what they are, insects of the spirit, worms of the soul. Skows, Richardsons and Mrazeks, how dare you make us suffer more who have suffered so much! You could not endure the thousand dangers we live with, nor the thousand horrors we die of. Your hearts could not bear that hideous strength which dwells within us.
>
> Keep your shameful lying selves elsewhere. You will never defeat us. We will never give up. With your millions and your power you may destroy us, but you will never defeat us. And if you come again and again, and ask for roaring war, we will bring it to your doorstep. We will not go gentle into that good night. We are the people of the Tongass.[13]

They like this passage so much that it appears twice, here in the middle of the book and then again, exactly the same, word processed, blocked, copied, and moved to the end.

"Here, let's go down into the cook shack where Jan Harbour's waiting for us. Have a cup of coffee. Let the heavy mood dissipate," begins the following section. That's all right with me. On the way I'm

13. People of the Tongass, 187-88 & 334.

going to be wondering where all this emotion is coming from, wondering if you gals might not find closer to home than the editorial offices of *Sports Illustrated* some folks with very ambiguous feelings about live loggers.

One of their more gratuitous rhetorical devices is to take printed words and put them back in their author's mouths and have them come out again as if the author hadn't been read but was being interviewed by the authors. The printed words of Lawrence W. Rakestraw's flattering (and funded by the Forest Service), "A History of the United States Forest Service in Alaska," appear in "People of the Tongass" as if transcribed from the authors' tape recorders. So how many levels of abstraction does that make? We read Rakestraw's words in "People of the Tongass" imagining that they have been spoken to the authors who wrote down what they heard. What they wrote down is actually not what they heard but what they read in "A History of the United States Forest Service in Alaska."

The other instance of print-to-speech-to-print is a case of what might be called textual incest. The publisher of the book, Ron Arnold, a leader in the "wise use" movement, steps out of his office and into the text, where some of his unpublished research on the enabling laws of the national forests is presented as if he were being interviewed:

> And for that [understanding] we turn to our editor Ron Arnold, who has uncovered previously unknown facts about the origin of the national forests.

> "It's unorthodox for an editor to intrude like this."

You made the discovery.
You tell the story

Ron Arnold's research, unsurprisingly, has uncovered a preservasionists' conspiracy. The shocking news is that it dates from 1891, almost a century of conspiracy ("People of the Tongass" was published in 1988).

They (now three, Arnold, DuRette and Soderberg) conclude their book by characterizing preservationists as selfish, snobbish, possibly racist, urban folk who have no legitimate claim to the forest, and who are actually immoral because they prefer plants and lower animals to people:

> All the opponents of our industrial base, the Sierra Club, Defenders of Wildlife, Environmental Defense Fund, Friends of the Earth, Western Federation of Outdoor Clubs, Wilderness Society, and National Parks and Conservation Association must be reformed from their present unethical intent and antisocial goals, by congressional action if necessary. To the extent they act to destroy the forest products industry, which is a responsible renewable resource industry, they are not friends of you or me or the earth we live on. If they will not be reconciled to a healthy thriving forest products industry they must be reconstituted along more humane lines or cut out of society altogether. To the extent that they exclude productive harmony and emphasize only enjoyable harmony, they are unethical and antisocial.
>
> In a word, the anti-industry aspect of environmentalism must be eliminated in favor of productive harmony.[14]

As rhetorical strategists the author's appear to have overdone by way more than half. If the audience was a limited one, say Alaskans who vote for Stevens, Murkowski, and Young, (each of

14. People of the Tongass, 327

whom wrote an introduction to the book) then the book would be a little locker room pep talk, something to hearten the home team, and the last chapter, addressed directly to the rest of us, is really there for their own folks to hear, and perhaps to admire the strategy. "You know how them environmentalists Down South do, serve 'em right to get a little of their own medicine."

But, there *is* textual evidence, of a sort, that Soderberg and DuRette are, at least in some moments, addressing a larger audience. Scattered through the text are references to muskegs, wetlands where trees don't grow. The authors wish to make the points that there are in the forest naturally unforested areas and tourists often mistake muskegs for clear-cuts. "If you flew over such small clear-cuts during their first years of regrowth you'd have a hard time distinguishing them from natural muskeg openings—and we frequently see folks looking out Alaska Airlines windows at natural muskeg, complaining 'look what those condemned loggers did!'"[15] The literal point of view from which the forest is seen in this passage is the point of view of almost all travelers to Southeast Alaska: five miles up. The point of view of travelers on the decks of ferries and cruise boats steaming up Chatham Strait is five miles off.

There are few roads and trails in Southeast Alaska, or in all of Alaska for that matter even counting logging roads; most travelers to and within Southeast, locals as well as visitors, cruise or fly from town to town. With that five-mile perspective, and with the whole forest as your place, it is easier to see how a logging operator, like K. D. Soderberg and her husband, Virgil, could move into a drainage, annihilate it and move on to another one with the belief that they are both still in their home place and haven't damaged it. This makes more comprehensible the curious suggestion made by K. D. and Jackie that we, "Pressure the Forest Service to allow timber harvest operations at appropriate places that are clearly visible to cruise ships, and to publish cruise ship brochures explaining what is actually happening, and where the many outstanding examples of forest regrowth are thriving."[16] It seems clear that they expect at least some of us

15. People of the Tongass, p.26.
16. People of the Tongass, p. 333.

from outside to share both their literal and figurative points of view.

Further evidence that their audience is outside Alaska is that they do not include SEACC, the Southeast Alaska Conservation Council in the above list of "opponents of our industrial base," nor "The Ravencall" as an ingredient of "the massive dose of media poison presently being penned against the resource users of the Tongass National Forest." Everybody in the Tongass knows that it is this group of Alaskans and their publication that proved to be most persuasive in getting Congress to take up the Tongass National Forest Reform Bill. They do get around to acknowledging them on page 326. "To discredit the most local and most vocal opponents of our industrial base in the Tongass is, thankfully, not terribly difficult. . . . Their pronouncements are less skillfully contrived than those of many environmental groups." Less skillful? It was their bill; they fought for it for eight years. It passed.

At The Second Annual North American Conference on Wilderness in Ogden, Utah in February of 1990, I made a presentation about "People of the Tongass" and another book about the region of the Northeast Pacific rainforest, "The Island Within" by Richard K. Nelson. Afterwards, in the five-minute discussion period, colleagues asked me, rhetorically, why I didn't just ignore Soderberg and DuRette. I responded that I was trying to understand the basis for their anger. *It*, I thought, was genuine. I didn't (and still don't) believe that it was only about money. Then fortunately my five minutes were up. I was at the very outer boundary of my clear thoughts about the book. I had not a sentence from the book to offer as evidence of their sincerity. Their multiple rhetorical stratagems make the text self-referential to a degree where it is difficult to find any unshifting ground, accept their anger, from which to venture into the argument. No fact or meaning of their text stands clear of the question of authorial intention. Or to put it plainly, you can't read a paragraph of "People of the Tongass" without wondering what the authors are up to now. Conspiracy thinking is contagious.

Master Logger of the Tongass

Sometime during the two day trip to Sitka by way of Skagway, chatting with Phil, enjoying the passage and the scenery, I remembered that Pat Soderberg lived in Sitka. I though I might recover some of the dignity lost in my panicked departure from Wrangell by talking to him. A friend had told me that Pat could get really angry at a person for no other reason than he thought him to be an environmentalist. In telephoning him for an interview, I mentioned that I had first learned about him from "People of the Tongass," co-authored by his daughter-in-law, and that I was using it that quarter in a course.

"Here he is," said the waitress in Staton's Steak House, Sitka, "that's his pickup." A white pickup parked right in front of the window beside my table. The window was slightly tinted. Because it was sunny and bright outside and cocktail-lounge dim inside, he could see in the glass only the reflection of the water behind him: so I was able to observe Pat Soderberg from a distance of eight feet without being seen as rudely staring at him. He was wearing a white windbreaker and light tan trousers. His hair was gleaming white but I could not guess how far beyond his late sixties he was. His walk, strong but measured and deliberate, led me to think that he might look younger than he is. He is also shorter than your average mythic figure, I thought, as I stood up to greet the man who opened up industrial logging in the Tongass. As we sat down, I explained further that I was a member of an interdisciplinary team whose topic was wilderness, and that with the Tongass bill and the owl controversy both in the air, I wanted to hear his views, of course, but more than that I wanted to know what his life had been like. His view was, "I'll tell you, I've never seen the US Forest Service do anything to lower the cost of logging." From cutting the size of the units that could be logged to requiring `non-violent' (no splash) log dumps, each new rule the Forest Service made about how logging is to be done on the Tongass made it more expensive. Nonetheless, he retired, not a poor man, "with no regrets." "I don't regret a single thing I've done in those twenty-five years." His view clear, we turned to the way it was to him.

Pat Soderberg was born in Florence, Oregon, a town well known to Northwesterners as a seaside destination. He logged there and elsewhere in the Northwest until 1960, when he came to Alaska to log for the Alaska Pulp Corporation. (APC is the Japanese corporation lured to the Tongass by the promise of a guaranteed wood supply at guaranteed prices, thus creating what the *New York Times* described as the acquisition of old-growth trees worth hundreds of dollars for the price of a McDonald's hamburger.) Pat came to the Tongass from Humboldt Bay, California by loading up two barges with his logging equipment ("all paid for") and headed up the coast with $150,000 in his logging account. "I had a letter of credit for $300,000 with APC and was down that plus another $200,000 before we got the money-flow turned around."

I'd heard that he had been responsible for several innovations in Tongass logging practices? Indeed he had. Their first site was Rodman Bay, at the northeast corner of Baranof Island, the island Sitka is on. They first developed a way to build roads on the grade, and then, "when the backhoe came along, we built the road on the debris." In light of Southeast Alaska's 100 plus inches of annual rainfall, and its muskegs, learning to build the roads on the debris created in making the road was probably the key innovation in enabling large-scale logging operations. The road is raised above the groundwater, and the rainwater drains easily through it.

My favorite of Pat's innovations is one where he outwitted the Forest Service's tendency to make logging more expensive. The Forest Service enacted the "non-violent dumping" policy in order to protect shellfish and the benthic layer. Logs could no longer be dumped into the water with a big splash. The Forest Service offered plans for a facility, a kind of a dock costing not much more than twenty-five thousand dollars. By experimenting, Pat found that a beach of 17°, with two logs laid down the beach to the water, made a ramp down which a log would roll into the water without making a splash.

I asked him if for him solving problems was the most interesting part of his work. "I believe so," he said, "I always enjoyed the rigging up (of a high lead). Most of all, I liked setting up camp, planning how to lay it out, putting in the water and the sewer—so that everything works in the winter as well as in the summer. Recreation. Not many people came up here and built *everything*, from scratch, with no outside help, no subsidies...or foodstamps like people in town. We even had to fly our own mail in."

Not all of his innovations were with rigging and construction. When Pat remarked that he never had any labor problems and he had crew that worked for him their whole logging careers, I asked him why he thought that was so. "I believe I had a pretty good idea of what loggers want—because I belonged to a couple of militant unions back in 1935-40, the Carpenters and Joiners Union and the IWA, International Woodworkers of America—they want a little job security. So for one thing we ran things on seniority, kinda, and we had a profit sharing plan. That was on top of their pension plan. Some of my people who worked for me twenty years or more got forty to fifty thousand out of that at their retirement, you know, added to their pension."

His ideal years, his best time?

"That would be Rodman Bay. Perhaps it was because we were younger and our kids were there, but there was a real sense of community for us there. We had a ball-field. We had a Center where they had Halloween Parties and such, you know, an old-fashioned good time. We had a movie every week. People were really interested in that. Everybody came. We really had a good time at the ball games. We never had a camp as good as Rodman Bay again. For one thing, there wasn't enough room. Rodman Bay was on an alluvial plain; there was room enough for a ball field."

I could see that he enjoyed remembering that time. I enjoyed imagining it myself. The future?

"Oh I really hated it for Virgil to give up logging. `Dad, I'll never log on public land again,' he said. I didn't try to influence him, I never have. He asked me about going to Viet Nam and I said I couldn't tell him what to do about that."

What does he guess Virgil will do? "Well, he's trying to sell his equipment now, this year. I hope he does. He probably will; then I think he might go into politics. He's real good at talking to people in public."

We went on to talk about getting older, staying active, enjoying retirement, and his boat. As we talked, I recalled a remark of John McPhee's in "Coming Into the Country," "Bust me to private in the army of environmentalists. I could not see the harm this man had done." Pat Soderburg had lived a life where he had not only done everything right, he had done it exceptionally well. I was moved by this man's life. In it was a story into which I was happy to be taken.

Smokey on Line

Pat's opening remark about the Forest Service called up his daughter's, "But when a cheechako carpetbagger like Skow comes Jet-hopping into our home for ten days, smilingly claims he's going to write 'a balanced article,' goes away an 'expert,' and then spouts malignant rubbish about the people of the Tongass to an audience of 19 million of our fellow Americans, we'll defend the Forest Service even if it sticks in our craw."[17] In the debate over the spotted owl, the Forest Service was enjoying something like a reprieve from the anger of both loggers and environmentalists. The fate of old growth timber is almost entirely within their hands, especially in Alaska, which has most of what's left of it. The chief target of Alaskan conservationists, and the specific topic of the Tongass National Forest Reform Act, (legislation passed subsequently after a ten-year battle to cancel 50 year contracts and millions in subsidies to the two pulp mills in Southeast Alaska) the Forest Service hardly figures in the public discourse about the spotted owl. The obvious reason that the Forest Service in Alaska is not a major player is because there are no spotted owls in the Tongass. The larger debate, the debate about what happens to what we have left of virgin timber, is being conducted within the Forest Service itself, on line.

The Forest Service has recently become divided within itself between biologists responsible for assessing the environmental consequences of cutting timber and those whose job it is to "get out the product." One of the points in common that Jock and his retired forester friend discovered was they were both readers of *The Inner Voice*.

17. People of the Tongass, P. 29

The Inner Voice is the publication of the Association of Forest Service Employees for Environmental Ethics, the association and paper was founded by a friend of Jock's, Jeff DeBonis. Jeff's first public words, uttered in print the Summer of 1989, were:

> Are you a frustrated Forest Service Employee because your resource ethics conflict with your job?
>
> Are you afraid to speak out for what you know is ecologically right?
>
> Do you feel isolated and alone because of your resource ethics?
>
> Do you think the Forest Service needs to become a more ecologically sensitive organization?
>
> Would YOU like to help promote this kind of change within the Agency?

Who are we?

We started out with two people. On a hot Saturday afternoon last September, a timber sale planner and a wildlife biologist were hiking through the Three Sisters Wilderness on the Willamette National Forest. We were discussing the frustrations of being a Forest Service Employee. The frustration over the agency's resource exploitation and its resulting contribution to world-wide environmental degradation and loss of bio-diversity. The frustration over the fact that as an agency, we could be LEADERS for a new resource ethic, instead of being followers of an out-dated, short-sighted agenda of the past. Frustration at the agency's continued denial that we are doing anything wrong, despite the public outcry and continuing litigation and losing of court cases and appeals. Frustration at the agency's attitude that our main mission is to supply raw wood products at any environmental cost to an industry that has already depleted it's own resources in the quest for the fast buck and good stock reports. We wondered out loud whether we should quit and go to work for a more socially and environmentally aware organization.

I first saw *The Inner Voice* on Nelson's desk, during the same trip where I discovered "People of the Tongass" and met Thomas Jack. When I first read the above, I thought that if there was a harbinger of the new world order, there couldn't be a better one than *The Inner Voice*. I was thinking about my own departure from the Park Service, a departure that would not have been necessary, I imagined, had there existed a vehicle such as this where I could voice my disagreements with the bureaucracy without being considered a traitor. I had hoped to meet Jeff DeBonis on my visit to see the spotted owl, but he was already, less than a year after the founding of AFSEEE, away on a speaking tour.

My estimate of the proximity of the new world order stretched out somewhat further into the future when, between the second and the third issue of *The Inner Voice*, Jeff De Bonis did leave the Forest Service and became himself an environmentally aware organization. Still, the critical medium of change introduced in the eight years between Jeff DeBonis's awakening and the founding of AFSEEE is still in place: the VDT terminals of "DG" (after Data General), the Forest Service's electronic mail network. The discourse now carried on in *The Inner Voice* began and continues on these screens. This venue is free of cost to the participants in the discourse, is unfettered by rhetorical tradition, requires no training, needs not to make a profit, carry advertisements, or be entertaining. It is about as free as speech of any consequence gets. It is difficult to censor. It is not impossible to censor, it still require's moral courage to participate in the discourse, but the discourse is almost as direct and immediate as that carried on in the agora. It is Hannah Arendt's "space of appearance" that "comes into being wherever men are together in the manner of speech and action," and is beginning to be listened to outside of the Forest Service. In the spring of 1992, the AFSEEE participated in the Protecting Integrity and Ethics Conference, and afterwards met with Congressional aides. The only way the hierarchy could forcibly prevent the Forest Service from reforming itself from within is to shut down its computers.

Designers of new bureaucracies with consciences, in addition to moral courage, will need insight. This too the Forest Service provides free, as I learned when I finally did get to meet Jeff and hear his story. The bureaucracy itself creates insight in the old fashioned way: by overreaching in its effort to prevent it.

Jeff DeBonis graduated in forestry from Colorado State University, and, after a hitch in the Peace Corps, prepared to spend his life protecting the nation's forests. Although a timber guy, not a biologist, he was startled by practices of clear-cut logging in Kootenai National Forest in Montana. His co-workers reassured him that what he was witnessing was "scientific forestry." This stuff had been studied for years, in the finest of facilities, by the most respected silvaculture scientists. Clear-cutting was actually good for the forest. Jeff soon became as "gung-ho a Timber Beast as any of them." He could have easily remained that way if it hadn't been for one mentally tough Forest Service wildlife biologist on the Kootenai, Ernie Garcia. This was 1980, Jeff's third year with the service. Ernie could not be made to back down in discussions about the damage they were doing to the forest by over-cutting and clear-cutting. There were also the laws protecting species and habitat, which he insisted upon calling to their attention. Jeff joined right in with the effort to bring Ernie around. After a while, Jeff began to wonder what was the matter with this guy. Why wouldn't he get with the program?

It wasn't Ernie's arguments, or his courage that finally persuaded Jeff to Ernie's position, it was the spectacle of his co-workers ganging-up on Ernie. Jeff got a whiff of the fear of the mob, the fear *within* the mob. "I suddenly saw what we were trying to do to him. I heard the denial. We were at him not because he was wrong but because he was right." Eight years later, Jeff and another wildlife biologist had the conversation described in the first issue of *The Inner Voice*.

Maybe AFSEEE and the Timber Beasts will work something out that will save what's left of the forest as forest, maybe not. AFSEEE has already done a great service to all who earn their daily bread

working in huge institutions with noble-sounding statements of mission, and practices that seem to have been designed as basic training
for the life of quiet desperation. A huge bureaucracy has been forced
to interrupt its normal routine of self-protection to participate in a
soul-felt discourse on ethics. The ethics they are discussing are not
confined to human affairs, organizational ethics, professional ethics,
and matters of character; but almost miraculously, at the heart of this
gigantic bureaucracy, there is a discussion that includes human responsibility to the rest of creation. God help them.

Out There

I was up there in Southeast Alaska, in the middle of what is left of the
creation, with a kayak; I ought to do something with that kayak other
than give it a ride on the ferry. Steve Reifenstuhl, biologist for the
North Regional Association for Aquaculture, had to make a trip by
skiff out to the outlet of Redoubt Lake. Redoubt Lake sits at the head
of the northernmost of the fjords on the ocean side of Baranof Island.
There are nine or ten fjords on that side, depending on how you make
your distinctions between "inlets," "arms" and "bays." He offered
me and my kayak a ride. This may not seem to be much of an ad-
vancement over giving my kayak rides on the ferry, but, as Steve was
kind enough to point out to me, "Once you are out there, you have to
get back." This lightsome observation came from a man half my age,
who had made by kayak a combined circumnavigation of Chichagof
and Baranof Islands, a span of over two degrees of longitude open
to the ocean forty percent of the time. The final sixty-five mile stretch
down the Gulf of Alaska side of Chichagof, into Salisbury Sound,
through the Whitestone Narrows, back to Sitka, he did in seventeen
hours. I found his observation less encouraging than he might have
hoped. I got ready, ready or not, and loaded my kayak onto his
company's big, stout, seaworthy, custom-designed, welded-alumi-
num skiff that evening.

I went down to the dock the next morning to find the skiff nowhere to be seen and my kayak sitting on the float. Tied to the dock

in calm weather, the skiff had foundered during the night. Were the gods trying to tell me something or what? Undeterred, Steve brought up another skiff:

Friday, 6 October 1990; Sitka to Lake Redoubt Inlet: Steve Reifenstuhl dropped me off at the outlet to Redoubt Lake, where the Sockeye project is taking place. He suggested that the next bay to the south might be a good place. And, after checking out a little hole-in-the-wall pond, I camped near the head of the suggested bay. I was dropped off at 1400 and ended up barely having time to rig my camp. I discovered that I left my notebook, journal and flashlight behind. So I am keeping a record on the back of this chart. It rained hard during the night and the little stream I camped beside started roaring.

I didn't have a tent either, but I had not forgotten that; it was with Connie in Wyoming. She was visiting our daughter and granddaughter and took her own accommodation.

I camped on a small shelf of land between the water and a cliff, an awkward place to get to from the land side. There were no bear tracks or spoor and not much of a trail. Nelson had been trying to teach me to become aware of bear economy and to camp in places where bears are loathe to invest their energy.

Saturday, 7 October 1990: The weather is not good but is nothing compared to what is being predicted, 45 knots. I debated making a run for it and decided not for two reasons....

The time of arrival of the next pulse of the weather being imprecise, the speed of these pulses being faster than I can paddle, I might get caught out on unprotected waters. Besides, I just got there. My journal record through Sunday is of the old American story of trying to make oneself a home in the woods. It is a record of fidgeting and worry: water, shelter, fire, and food. Is that bear sign? It takes me a long time to settle into a place made by God and not by people. I was unable to escape from my own consciousness, my own tiny, personal concerns. It wasn't until midday Sunday, that I was able to look around for reasons other than to gain some advantage for myself. Two full days—and that starting from Sitka, which if you look at it on the map you will note is not exactly the center of the industrialized world—is actually not bad time. Northbound from Kauai on a 35' sailboat, it happened perhaps a few hours earlier, but it is surprising how long it takes for the natural rhythms of the earth to displace the beat we have drummed into ourselves by which to march, think, breathe and pump blood in time with our machines.

There is an account that has to be kept when you are figuring out if you are within your rights in being here. Did I earn the right to be here by the manner of getting here? No. I came most of the way by skiff. Hardship? Some, lots of rain; a bear might show up for the Sockeye run. Doing it right? Not as pure as Muir, but a tarp in place of a tent is worth a few points. I paddled myself the rest of the way here and will paddle my way out. Muir was paddled by natives. On the other hand his paddlers may have wanted him here. He had to be more fun to be with than the missionaries, though probably not so amusing a spectacle as they. Did Muir pay his paddlers? I don't re-member hearing.

I had no spiritual mission there that I was aware of. I had no inter-est in imagining myself living "subsistence," as they say in that coun-try. I foraged one mussel. That I was trying to "get back to the earth," I will not deny. However, I was not looking to get my hands dirty, or bloody, to build me up a sweat, nor was I in need of therapy, al-though I was happy to have it.

I suppose I thought of myself as looking for a plausible story about a possible future because I had not heard any good stories of that sort except the extinction story. Now the extinction story is a very persua-sive story; but it is not a story about the future; it is the story about the end of the future. The contending stories I'd been hearing are about what we do on our way to our end. Cut all the old growth and just see what happens next or don't do that? Drown ourselves in our own toxins or stop doing that? I accept Pat Soderberg's daughter-in-law's implied description of the moral choice: use for humans or pres-ervation for the sake of itself. Alaska needs not to be "set-aside," possible later use implied, it needs to be locked-up, us locked-out. *Period*, as she would say. Nobody back in until the world population drops by, say, twenty percent. Granted, those are the fair terms. Still, however small my claim on the place, until the logging of old-growth is stopped I am not locked-out. I was there on Alaska's outer coast in the early fall not because I should be but because I could be.

I had a day and a half out of time's arrow, half of Sunday and all of Monday, and then it was time to head back.

Tuesday, October 9, 1990; Lake Redoubt Inlet, SW Lobe to M/ V Columbia outbound from Sitka: Awoke at 0530 after a night of waking cold. Finally figured out the warmest position, and slept for two more hours. It was sunny, almost a cloudless sky and flat calm. Surge scarcely noticeable. The question of the morning was what to do with all the wood I dried. I finally took one straight-grain stick of cedar, my lucky stick, and a fire-starter bundle of twigs—this all in case I couldn't get around Cape Burunof and had to set up camp again. Breakfast, breaking camp, stashing the wood, a second cup of coffee, loading the kayak, eating a mussel, took two hours. Paddling to the islet in front of Dick and Nita's took exactly four hours, an extremely interesting four hours. The day was so beautiful, the new snow dusting the peaks so spectacular—I love the buckskin color of the vegetation above tree line—that I had to look up the names of the peaks to the SSE and to the N of the inlet. They are, respectively, Camel Mountain and Mount Dramishmikov. I successfully determined to remember the latter name; the former is so easy in comparison that it's a memory freebie. Of Camel Mountain Steve remarked on the way in that you could hike and camp along its ridges for five days. My attention eventually turned to Povorotni Point. I looked in vain for an obvious way through the white explosions of surf, brilliant in the sunlight, the white the only harsh color in the environment. The white of gulls, Bald Eagles, even the

white on a loon's throat seems bright against the softened
colors of the northern rainforest autumn. As I got to the
point, I first went up a blind alley, was about to give up
trying to find a way through Povorotni Point's rocks, when
the way opened up. It turned out to be a lure into a maze.
Maybe I made the wrong choice, but when I exited from
the maze, I got considerably tossed around, splashed, and
scared by waves crashing on rocks only two paddle-lengths
away from me. (Later I realized that I had forgotten to
connect the shoulder straps of my cockpit skirt and hadn't
cinched up the top so some water got below.) When I
looked across the bay to Cape Burunof, as compared to
the stuff breaking on the rocks protecting the route inside
along the beach, I decided to head straight across the entrance of the bay. Also, there was nothing but white spray
in the passage Steve came through on Friday. The swells
were big but there was almost no wind. A cloud that had
built around Mount Edgecombe on Kruzof Island showed
signs of detaching itself. So it went. Breaking swells shoreward, and, after a time, no obvious passage in; sea conditions changing, influenced by reefs to seaward and the bottom; the impossible cape ahead and weather brewing on
Kruzof. Eventually, I committed to go wide, actually, stay
wide. I was sorry that I hadn't put my anorak back on
before I got wet, sorry that I hadn't worn my wetsuit, but
I just felt more comfortable out in deep water where the
waves were more-or-less regular.

As I got nearer to being abeam of the cape, I realized
that it was possible to get on the back of a breaking wave
and not know it until it was too late.

This journal entry does not make explicit what the dramatic tension of the event being recorded actually was. It might be useful to
have that clear before getting on to the breaking wave.

Safety in this circumstance lay in getting offshore, moving out towards the open sea. I knew that; I said it out loud to myself. Every

sailor knows that the land, any ground, sand and mud as well as rock, is far more dangerous to the vessel than the sea. However, there was another fact of equal and opposite weight: I simply did not want to go further out toward the open ocean. My head knowledge about the direction of safety didn't have much traction against the bias, one might even say strong prejudice, I had shoreward. The result was that though I turned my bow a few degrees seaward, my eyes had a tendency to look towards the shore. The resulting course of the kayak was a kind of compromise which worked out about as compromises always seem to.

It turns out that much that interesting and important that you want to do in the world is like learning to do friction climbing. About two score years ago, on a crisp but sunny New Hampshire autumn day in that quiet color time between riotous leaves and eye-burning white of snow, I learned to friction climb on a slab of lovely, gray, close-grained, tombstone-quality granite. "Owl's Head" it was called, because the face of an owl had been formed on the cliff. Centuries of water freezing and wedging hairline cracks through the granite formed broad detachable slabs several feet thick, held by friction until the weight of the slab, at the instigation of one little last pry from a thin film of ice, dropped tons of granite to the boulder field below. The slabs had come off in great arches on either side, leaving protruding, overhanging brows with a pointed beak between them.

I never heard an expert account of why the slabs were wedged off from the bottom up, so I made up my own. The vegetation on top slows the passage of the leaching rain and stores it up until saturation, when it begins running down the face, picking up volume from the rain falling on the face itself, the lower down the face, the more water until some of the water has no place to go but inside the cracks, including uphill inside the cracks, which you can imagine it doing while the cracks are thin, no wider than a drop of water. The vegetation at the top also protects its water from freezing in the fall nights; water would freeze first on the face, the heavy cold night air descending into the valley from the heights lifting the warmer air above it, freezing water on the face from the bottom up. These conditions would appertain only a few nights a year, the autumn nights between the brilliant leaves and the snow, and a few nights in times of winter thaws. Only a few nights a year, but a few nights a year over all the time that there is, add up.

I made this nature story up while waiting for Peter Robinson, who was teaching me to climb, to finish a lead. I didn't tell him my story because he was a geologist and might not understand it.

The climb on Owl's Head was my first climb on anything other than the little ledges around Hanover. Like most beginning male climbers, my notion of technique was to seek out the best hand hold I could find in the near neighborhood, take a firm grip on it and haul myself up. Much later, when I began teaching climbing, I learned that women climbers, having less arm strength, know from the beginning the importance of balance and climbing mainly with their feet. I would use footholds, but footholds were nothing in the way of making me feel secure compared to a clutch hold on Momma Earth.

When we came to the slab, where there were suddenly alarmingly few handholds, Peter said, "This is the Friction Pitch," and glided across the slab with his hands resting on the air in front of him. Not me. I stooped down until I could get my hands on something anchored to the core of the planet and then awkwardly, my feet nervously interfering with each other, moved. The slab dropped out of sight below into a background of small, altitude-shrunk trees that had been much bigger when we walked through them on the approach. Although I was roped, Peter was almost straight across from me; if my feet slipped, and they were giving me signals that they might well just do that, I would go rolling and scraping, penduluming in an arc down to a point below him the length of the rope between us. It would hurt me; and I would probably utter something silly like, "I'm falling," not in a manly baritone either, but a squeak.

Inevitably, there were no more handholds of any kind on the slab, the unthinkable below me, and the roof of an overhang above my head. "You have to stand-up, get your weight over your feet, and relax," said Peter, "it's really quite easy once you get the hang of it."

He was right. All of my teachers have been right, it is easy once you get the hang of it. In skiing straight down the fall line in deep snow on a steep slope, in ice climbing, in giving a talk to an audience of strangers, in keeping a marriage going, as in friction climbing, once you release your grip on whatever you've been keeping a strangle-hold on, breathe easy, let everything go but balance and then go with it, it is easy. It'll be like that when we get right with the planet. It'll be like that when I finally learn to eskimo roll my kayak, too, I'm sure.

Knowing how to eskimo roll a sea-kayak might have given me psychological aid in what was to transpire but would have been of no practical utility:

9 October (continued): I watched a patch of foam ahead, won-dering what caused it. I went through it ok but no wiser. My course was a passage between a reef to the west and a rock island off the Cape. I noticed that the current of the flood tide seemed to want to push me toward the rock island. I pointed the bow more to the north but was lax about my heading and the set. All of a sudden one of the big swells [the one I happened to be on] rose up into a steep wall. Inexperienced though I am as a surfer, it was obvious that it was going to break. It did, not fifteen feet behind my 17 foot boat, me paddling like hell to get to the north and to get off its back. I'll remember for some time the roar of its breaking and the spray explosion I got a glimpse of out of the corner of my eye as the wave slammed into the island. That was the closest call, other than in an automobile, that I have had for some time—closest ever at sea. Somewhat shaken, I looked over toward Kruzof. The squall had moved out onto the water but seemed to be head-ing south. I remember a couple of those squalls in Nelson's skiff, and I sure did not want to be in the way of one of those. All in all, the water looked best right down the cen-ter of East Channel, but I felt I'd used up my luck on water open to the Gulf of Alaska, so I went behind Long Island as recommended by Steve. I arrived at Nelson's, the skiff on its mooring, the car there, but no sign of life at the house.

There was life at the house; its flame dimmed somewhat. Nelson was prone on the couch, with just enough energy to wonder if I had perished in Sunday's storm, but not enough energy to be able to lift his head above the back of the couch to look out the window to see if I was entering the harbor. He had the flu.

"You had about two more hours," he threatened weakly, "then we would have started searching."

"Sure," I said, "you couldn't even crawl to your skiff."

"We could have sent the Coast Guard," was the feeble rejoinder.

If there had been any rescuing, it would have been either the Coast Guard or the women. The men of the crew there in Sitka were not in good shape. Mark Gorman and Robert Rose also had the flu; Steve might also have had it, they hadn't heard from him; John Straley was out of town. At a dinner on Sunday evening, the guys had performed their accustomed male bonding ritual, all spooning ice cream out of the same container. None of the women got the flu. Nita was resting upstairs as a preventative measure to keep herself from getting it. She could have been ready if Ethan would take care of Nels, but she would have had to miss her soccer match that evening. Jan Straley, a whale researcher, had more time tooling skiffs around Alaskan waters than any of the men. She might have been willing if she could have found a babysitter for young Finn. Steve's wife, Andrea Thomas, leads kayaking and mountaineering expeditions in the summer for one of the more successful hoods in the woods programs. She would have been good, and was an Evergreen graduate, so might have been willing for old times sake. Carolyn Servid, a Greener from the pioneering class at Evergreen, wondering if I was going to make the ferry, stopped by a few moments after I hit the beach. She recently replaced the leaky rubber raft, with which she used to watch whales, with a beautiful little wooden dory. This dory, though slow, would have made an attractive addition to the flotilla. There was a task force of rescue vessels available to take over for the men debilitated by the rigor of their rituals. It would have made a fine story, but all in all, I was happier not to have needed rescuing.

I hadn't seen Nelson since he stopped by in Olympia the previous November, enroute to bookstores in points south and east to promote his just published, "The Island Within." "The Island Within" is Nelson's story about, among other things, what, during his twenty-five years as an anthropologist, he learned from Native Americans about an ethical relationship with nature. Nelson's view is that we can learn from the Athabaskans and Inuit, but we cannot borrow or steal from them. We have learned from them *that* it can be done, that humans can live on the planet without destroying or domesticating it, but they can't tell us how we can do it. From this much knowledge only, we have to make our own stories. The stories Nels made won for him the John Burroughs Award for Nature Writing.

The ferry was in and would be leaving in a couple of hours to catch the high slack in Sergius Narrows. We had time to get in an hour of conversation about his current work, a book on deer. When I arrived in Sitka the previous week, Nelson was off doing research. He had, over the last couple of months talked with eight scientists doing one kind or another of deer study. The deer is Nelson's favorite animal, "my totem animal or something." After getting the scientific stuff from the scientists, he asked each of them about their special feelings for the deer that led them into their research. He got the same answer in all eight cases, there are none. They each said that it wouldn't have mattered what animal had ended up being their subject, they were interested in the questions. He was surprised, not that Nelson didn't know that theory is all—animals are studied either below the level of the whole organism for their bio-chemistry, or above the level of the individual animal for their species behavior—he was surprised that neither the animals nor the species engaged their researchers on any level other than the analytical.

Another permutation of this same story is told by the naturalist, Steve Herman. Steve was up in the forest on the lower slopes of Mount Rainier on a field trip with students. If there is anything Steve likes to find in the field more than the animals that belong there it is a person who knows those animals. So, when he encountered at the side of a mountain stream a graduate student watching a water ouzel with good binoculars, he walked up to her and said, "I see you are watching a water ouzel. It is a nice bird to study isn't it?" She drew herself up and with scornful icy professionalism said, "I am *not* studying water ouzels, I am studying competitive exclusion." At that Herman, thoroughly chastened, retreated speechlessly into the forest.

Nelson seemed to gather strength, or at least agitation, as we continued our talk. He reached down into the box of reprints at his side and read from the methods and materials section of one journal article the sentence: "Nine adult mule deer were starved to death in three groups."[18] In context, with its technical language and careful, disciplined periods in passive voice make that sentence all the more frightening. We should not, in this time of massive species extinction, be surprised to find these signs of denial of our common destiny with the animals. Nelson has no plans to use these illuminating tidbits to chastise the individual scientific researchers he has talked to and read. They play the game according to the rules by which we want them to play. We know and expect the rules of the science game to discourage researchers from admitting to noticing, for example, that deer have lovely eyes. It might not be so good, however, if our rules made it impossible for researchers to imagine what it might be like, subjectively not objectively, to be a trapped and domesticated animal dying from starvation in a barren and overcrowded habitat. It might be a story worth remembering.

There was a strange-looking ship of a type I had never seen before, anchored in the harbor in front of Nelson's house. It looked to me like a cross between a tanker and a log ship. That turned out to be a good guess. As I got up to leave, I asked Nelson about it. "I call that the 'Dachau Boat'," said Nelson. "That's the ship that carries the wood pulp from the mill. That's the ship that is transporting the forest of the Alexander Archipelago to Japan."

Carolyn and Nita got me and my kayak to the ferry and I sailed back to the college wiser somehow. It had been proven that I'm no John Muir and the present seemed clearer if no less troubling. I carried no new word from the frontier, but—at a time in life when most of my existential encounters between my mortality and the creation take the form of complaints from my well-worn body—I had achieved one of those rare summits of recognition that gleam like peaks suffused in alpenglow above the ordinary landscape of darkening memory. When I broke the grip of the curling crest and the bow slipped quietly and gracefully down the back of the breaking wave, I remembered once more that there is life and all the rest is mere abstraction. With right or not, I am here: I crest the cold, sunlit, salt sea, laughing.

18. "Some Effects of Starvation on Mule Deer Rumen Bacteria," Journal of Wildlife Management, vol. 38, No. 4 (1974) 815-22.

Back to Town

An advantage of professing at a small liberal arts college that approves interdisciplinary study and team teaching is that my colleagues constitute a living, self-revising encyclopedia. My friend, entomologist, population ecologist, and evolution theorist, Dr. Robert Sluss, has been my personal consultant on his subjects for the two and a half decades we've been on our faculty together. Bob rereads "Moby Dick" annually and, with his bewhiskered jowls and equability, is noted among his colleagues for his resemblance, physically and psychologically, to Stubbs, the second mate of the "Pequod." Like Stubbs, Bob smokes a pipe; also like Stubbs he reaches for it when he debunks in the morning. Whereas Stubbs has a loaded rack of pipes at hand, "lighting one from the other to the end of the chapter; then loading them again to be in readiness anew," Bob's pipes are ever misplaced—and when by chance his pipe is at hand it's "now I've lost my tobacco."

Bob and I enjoy guessing about what will limit human population. Bob persuaded me that not only should I use the elevators instead of the stairs, but, in order to use up as much energy as possible, I should push the button to call the elevator whenever I walk by the button panel. I can't consistently adhere to this practice, surrounded as I am by hundreds of policing environmentalists, but I am persuaded by his argument that using up energy is a more humane way to limit our population than exhausting food, space, or resistance to disease. Bob's latest theme is that "environmental management is presently the number one threat to ecological stability and environmental integrity."

Bob's views have mellowed over the years, though only his friends can tell it. Robinson Jeffers is still his favorite poet and his favorite poem is "Birds and Fishes" which ends:

> The wings and the wild hungers, the wave-worn skerries,
> the bright quick minnows
> Living in terror to die in torment—
> Man's fate and theirs—and the island rocks and immense ocean

beyond, and Lobos
Darkening above the bay: they are Beautiful?
That is their quality not mercy, not mind, not goodness,
but
the beauty of God.

Twenty years ago, Bob was a proponent of nuclear energy because humans suffer the adverse effects of radiation poisoning before most other species of animal and plants. "A dose of radiation fatal to humans if concentrated entirely on the testes of a cockroach will just barely sterilize it," Bob gleefully explains, "that's what 'The meek shall inherit the earth' really means." In his mellowing he has become expansive to the point where he is a proponent of almost any form of pollution.

"Pollution is one of the ways that nature responds as populations reach their carrying capacity," says Bob. "All species cause environmental alterations that are harmful to their welfare. Living organisms produce wastes that are harmful to themselves and other organisms, and/or they produce parasites, pathogens and predators that are harmful to themselves and other organisms, and/or they use up some essential resource faster than it is produced. It is these self-produced harmful effects that set limits to the population sizes of species. In the case of other species, we call the results natural control that leads to the balance of nature; in the case of ourselves, we call the results environmental problems to be solved.

"Environmental agencies assume that what is good for us is good for the environment: an untenable notion when you consider that they exist at all because of what humans have done to the environment. In view of our relationship to the environment, a notion that what is harmful to us is good for the environment, is much more justified."

Our thinking about pollution is the result of our inability to think of nature as it is instead of as ours. Bob points out that we who live on Puget Sound attend to the coliform count in the sound as folks in L.A. do the air particulate count. "Of all the pollutants that human activity puts into the Sound," observes Bob, "human waste is the one most legislated against and tested for. By clearing the Sound of human waste, they make it safe for clam, oyster, and other shell fish harvesting and a variety of other aquaculture. Aquaculture, like its terrestrial counterpart, agriculture, makes pests out of many of the organisms that normally live in the environment: oyster drills, moon snails, starfish, scaup ducks, herons, grebes and other clam or fish eating birds. Human waste, in addition to protecting clams, oysters and their predators from human harvesting and management is, like seal, fish, and bird waste, nutrients for the planktonic organisms that form the basis of productivity in the Sound ecosystem. The idea of total human waste abatement is simply another effort to turn the entire ecosystem into human production. Success will destroy the environment at a much greater rate than will a bit of feces."

I understand Bob's story to mean that Nature goes about her business indifferent as to whether our population is limited by a dignified maturity and decline to a decent sustainable level or by a frightening series of catastrophic bursts of overgrowth and crashes, it's all the same to her. Nature thinks that Manhattan is for cockroaches as well as humans; productivity is productivity. We may, as our Yankee poet says, "have ideas yet we haven't tried," but they are nothing compared to what nature has ready, tried and untried, and waiting for us to move on. Just because we keep the list does not mean that we are not also an endangered species.

From our point of view as individual organisms in an ecosystem, a condition of relative stability in the system is desirable. Says Bob:

> Since just one thing can not be changed in an ecosystem, a way to achieve populations varying between their normal ranges is to value diversity. Maintenance of normal diversity is generally assumed to lead to maintenance of relative stability in an ecosystem. Normal diversity means that populations are left to fluctuate normally over time, and that the complex of those population fluctuations over time make an ecosystem what it is. This is the case for all populations making up the ecosystem, because as soon as one population exceeds either its normal upper limit or its normal lower limit, one or more other populations will either

be displaced or expanded in response to those changes,
and that in turn will have further repercussions.[19]

Nature, a wanton lover of life, loves indiscriminately, plays no
favorites, will not be domesticated. Indifferent to the concerns of particular individuals or species, nature does have a bias toward relative
stability in an ecosystem. Nature limits populations not diversity, which
is what we try to limit. The human species pretends it has no limits
and thinks no more of diversity than the diversity of what it regards
as its needs, species of plants and animals to feed, clothe and heal us.
Humans cannot be blamed for their nature any more than ants theirs,
but it is something of a burden to be a member of the only species in
creation that doesn't have its own niche and so has opted for, in the
words of Bill Kittredge, *Owning It All*.

As Bob and others have observed, "Native Americans did what they
could to influence the environment for their own welfare: game management, controlled burning, and a host of religious/spiritual stratagems. They had a better ecological relationship to the environment
than did the invading Europeans and our current dominant culture,"
because, "the environment was less favorable to themselves than it was
to the invaders." The European stratagems to influence the environment produced increased carrying capacities and higher rates of increase of population than did the stratagems of the native Americans.
It is worth knowing that some groups such as the Athabaskans of the
Boreal Forest, lived on the land for certainly 10,000 years and possibly
as many as 30,000 years, leaving no permanent sign of their being
there. While it seems, at this point anyway, that there is no going back,
it is instructive to know about our species that it is not inherent in our
nature to destroy our habitat. While it is inherent in our nature to try to
influence our habitat, peoples who do so by spiritual means are rewarded by a habitat undamaged by themselves at least, if not undamaged by volcanic eruption and glacier.

Bob's grievance with environmentalists stems from their claims to
know better what to do about the environment. It is this intellectual
failure, especially we who are educated and privileged, that drives Bob
to strong language, such as: "Environmentalists are the single greatest

19. From the author, unpublished paper, October 1990.

threat to the environment we now have." The threat is that 1) they choose to ignore the role of pollution in an ecological system, 2) they don't accept limits, and 3) they choose use over enjoyment of nature.

The role of pollution in setting limits is a simple empirical observation. We can be expected to note and understand that we will produce pollutants detrimental to ourselves. Accepting that our population will eventually thus be limited is harder to swallow—imagining what it will be like to be limited does not come easily to us. Seattle is the number one recycling city in the world. Is this an indication that Northwesterners are willing to make do, to accept limits? I think not. It is instead evidence of our confidence in our management efforts.

When Bob was a young Department of Agriculture entomologist giving advice to farmers on natural controls, he learned that the only thing you couldn't tell them is to not do anything. We *will* manage the environment, says Bob, "It is not possible for people to voluntarily accept lack of health or to desist conservation efforts (raising the carrying capacity), but it is possible to recognize that we make such efforts because we have to and to stop trying to pass them off as efforts to save the environment."

Given his observation that we can't not do something, why can we not try to manage wetlands for wildlife production, under the pretext of managing them for our benefit, hoping that the correction to our population growth will overtake us before we overrun the wetlands? Bob addressed this question indirectly, "We need an absence of management for the enjoyment of nature. Enjoyment here is used here in the sense introduced by St Augustine, i.e. the love of something for its own sake, as he suggests we are to 'enjoy' God." He concludes:

> I believe that the only effective solution to environmental problems is to get large amounts of land out of human use (other than observation), and out of human management. The most likely way to accomplish this is for people to learn to enjoy nature and the best way to do that is to stimulate interest in natural history. You can not enjoy what you do not know. Tree lovers, wolf lovers, bird lovers, bug lovers, and whale lovers, consist of people who

know about those things—maybe not all the whale lovers, many of them seem to like whales because they think
they are just like us.[20]

Bob's story, the story of population ecology, is most persuasive in
its account of the past and present, but it ends at the point where
we'd like to have some hope for the future. Getting large amounts of
land out of human use certainly would keep our management skills
honed. It could easily turn into a major defense industry as we would
need to build walls keeping us out which would need to be as secure
as the Berlin Wall and several times the length of the Great Wall of
China. Unfortunately, what evidence we have suggests that it is probably better for the planet in its traditional form, the one we evolved
into, for us *not* to resist our anyway nearly irresistible urge to catch
the last wild salmon and cut down the last wild tree. This urge we
have to use up or domesticate everything is probably the shortest and
cleanest route to reaching a limit on our population, and is, then, the
best management system if efficiency is the point of having a management strategy. Which is our highest value, management for
management's sake or using it all? We are about to find out.

The best look into the future is that of our colleague Tom Grissom,
physicist, poet, and recovering weapons builder whose former em-
ployment was at a National Laboratory. Tom's 1990 Christmas present
to his brother was a copy of "Chaos: Making a New Science" by
James Glieck. Tom included with his gift a clear and useful account
of chaos theory and its consequences. First explaining the consequential differences between linear and non-linear equations and systems—
the latter are unpredictable, counter-intuitive, and irreversible—Tom
turns to the practical environmental consequences of the theory:

> Once natural systems are altered, they do not come back
> exactly as they were before. The dinosaurs disappeared,
> and we shall not see them again. We are at present making
> irreversible changes in the environment, on a global scale
> never before witnessed in our recorded history. The long-
> term consequences are unpredictable, as are the conse-
> quences of our actions aimed at trying to undo the envi-

20. From the author, unpublished paper, October 1991.

ronmental damage, making the warning of chaos theory
ring ominous.

Faced with this reality, the prudent course would be to
minimize our actions—all of our actions—those which tend
to alter the natural systems of our environment, and those
otherwise well-intentioned ones designed to correct and
reverse the changes already incurred.

Tom too doesn't think that "this reality" is going to be any more
efficacious in teaching us to restrain our inherent propensity to futz
with things than the threat to take away our toilet-paper has been in
stopping the Nature Conservancy from setting aside land. "We are most
of all unlikely to sit idly by and do nothing in the face of some perceived threat, for it is a constant component of the human condition
that we are forever faced with the necessity to act in a world of limited
understanding. When Camus summarized his own view, saying. 'But I
have always held that, if he who bases his hopes on human nature is a
fool, he who gives up in the face of circumstances is a coward,' he
spoke to something very basic in the collective consciousness."

There is hope of a sort in Tom's physical view similar to the hope
in Bob's biological view, the plausibility of there being limits that we
cannot get around. As Tom says: "With the advent of chaos, the epis-
temology of 20th century physics has come full circle. The early part
of the century brought relativity and quantum mechanics, limiting
forever what we can know about the cosmos and the microcosm respectively." He explains:

Thus far, we have told ourselves that it is only our unique
size that limits us. If we had been as large as a galaxy we
would have discovered relativistic physics first, and the
strange phenomena associated with motion near the speed
of light would conform to our intuition. If we has been as
small as an atom, then quantum mechanics would seem
the appropriate description of the world. Instead we are
trapped somewhere in between, excluded by our size and
the laws of nature from being able to directly experience
either the cosmos or the microcosm, Now the new science

of chaos tells us that the limitation is no longer one of size only. Even the world we directly experience is inherently unpredictable and, to that extent, unknowable. "The limits to human knowledge" has become the constant and universal theme of science in the 20th century. Long after the initial excitement over new applications has passed, that may be the most enduring lesson of chaos.

Although we now know, as surely as we know the constant for the speed of light, and by the same means, mathematical insight, that we cannot manage the planet in any meaningful sense of the word because we can never know enough, we just do not yet believe it. It is possible we will never believe it. While there may be an absolute limit to what we know, there seems to be no such limit to what we can contrive to believe. Still, experience, that which has happened to us about which we have a story to tell—has some limiting effects on our imaginations, effects tending toward modesty. Most of us experience limits of many kinds and numerous failures to manage. "Experience, though noon auctoritee/ Were in this world, were right y-nough to me/ To speke of wo that is in mariage," says Chaucer's Wife of Bath. Specifically, experience, though suspect as an avenue to knowledge, has a powerful effect on what we believe. Most of us, though capable of great feats of imagining, tend to be quite conservative about what we believe when it comes to actually doing something. That conservative streak might be almost enough to save the last of the ancient forests. It is one thing to believe that human technological inventiveness is practically unlimited. That has been our experience. It is quite another thing to expect us to believe that we can destroy something as big and complex as a forest or a marriage and then, with the help of our inventiveness, put it back together again. It's been a long time since I've heard anyone bragging about their marriage contract.

The trouble with cautionary experiences is that they come when such experiences actually make us afraid. Because courage is the preferred response to fear, fear only makes us that much more eager to manage, to gain control, to brave the future. What hope we have for sustaining set-asides will not result from threatening ourselves about our survival. Our hope depends on the political and moral authority of those who argue for set-asides. Their argument must include all in the proscription. Though we environmentalists might gain enough political power to roll over the loggers or even the timber industry, we have no moral authority unless we can demonstrate that we enjoy the forests (or plains, or deserts, or shores) out of love alone.

The paradox resides in the facts that, as Bob says, "we are unlikely to love what we don't understand," on one hand, and what a few hundred millions of us learning to love nature would do to her on the other. Does nature mean only the wilds; can't it mean sheep are in the pasture, cow's in the barn, posies in the window box, and the odor of manure freshened by the smell of new mown hay? No it can't mean those. Nature now has to mean wilderness, not the garden, because agriculture was the start of the trouble, the prime transgression, "the Neolithic Catastrophe" as the anthropologist Hugh Brody is wont to call it. Wilderness is the "Other" of agriculture; until agriculture there was no wilderness, the whole shebang was the garden. What's left of that garden we must stay out of, not because of the cherubs, and the flame of a flashing sword, but out of love. Because the unequivocal proof of love is willingness to relinquish possession of the beloved, if the users can't go into the set-asides we lovers can't go in. If we can't love the wild without being in it, then Soderberg and DuRette, however self-serving their motives for their argument, have got it right: that we're in it only for the esthetics, or worse, the therapeutics; and we are indeed non-ethical if not exactly unethical. What would happen to the unemployed naturalists and environmental impact statement writers? We could put them to work back in town, making the cities habitable.

Back in Town

Mark Papworth, friend and colleague, anthropologist, archeologist, sometime forensic pathologist, deputy sheriff in Thurston, Mason, and Lewis counties, deputy coroner, serial-killer investigator, investigator of "old homicides," teaching-by-television personality, hunter, fisherman, motorcyclist, powerboater—above all collector, and raconteur of stories old and new—has his office across the hall from mine. I told him about my difficulties with getting clear about wilderness and finding the right story.

I said that I had been looking for a story about a possible future that would not be news, information, or entertainment—distractions all three seem to be now; would not be shamanistic (he being an anthropologist I thought he might like that word) in any of the ways we tell shamanistic stories: science, political philosophy, economics, or theology; would be public knowledge rather than privileged knowledge; and would have the verifiability of fiction—where you can tell if it's right even if you haven't exactly experienced it. I filled him in on my wanderings east and north.

He said, "You want a story? I know a guy who's got the best story ever. This is the best story of this century. His name is Perry Squyres; he lives right here in Olympia; I'll introduce you to him some time." Mark then told me Perry's story, told it to me again four months later in February, and one more time in April. Here is a composite version of those tellings. This version is, as were Mark's three versions, much like the story I got from Perry, except that Mark melded together two of Perry's hunting stories. I like the effect Mark got by doing that. Perry is planning to write his own version of his story, so I'll let him tell that one. A written story never seems to come out like the talk story, the one that is "performed" as the social scientists say. There is but one line of the story that has to be exactly right in writing and speech. I use Perry's version of that line. The story belongs to all of us; tell it yourself as best you can.

The Best Story of the Twentieth Century: The Papworth Variation

Perry and his buddy Bill Watson, who still lives in New Mexico, were born in the early years of the Depression. Bill was born in 1927 in Coleman, Texas. They were in high school together in Carlsbad, in New Mexico, which in those days was still mainly wild country on the high ground between the Pecos and Rio Grande Rivers, high plains and exposed desert rock formations, supporting desert wildlife. Perry is a hunter of the old school, the million or so years of our evolution before hunting became sinful. His house is loaded with trophies, an animal rightist's nightmare.

So there are these two high school guys, Bill and Perry, back at the time near the end of the war. Perry and Bill worked the country around them every chance they got. They were either hunting, fishing, or looking for places to hunt and fish in all the time they had after working and school. They particularly liked to hunt wild turkey, they were in one of the few places in the country where you could. One day while scouting around in the desert down there around Carlsbad, they located a roosting spot, a copse of cottonwoods down in a draw, feathers scattered around underneath, the tops of the branches white with the guano. The best way to hunt turkeys is to find one of these roosting sites and sneak up to it in the last dark of the night. You wait till dawn, when the turkeys start fluttering down out of the trees. You wait to fire until you can see the one you want. It is not as easy as it sounds.

To pay for gas for his Model A sports roadster, Perry had a job at a Firestone store. He worked after school and stayed on after closing time to clean up. On Saturday night, when folks came into town, the store closed at nine. Bill, who worked at the Caverns, got off earlier, so he came by around six to pick up Perry's car. Then he loaded their shotguns, hunting jackets and gear into Perry's car, made up a couple of sandwiches and a thermos of coffee, and went back to the station to get Perry. They made their way out across the plains toward the

Guadelupe Mountains, opening and closing gates, flushing rabbits in their headlights, and one badger, bouncing along, springs creaking, the stars dropping down toward them as they got up into the thinner air, until they got to the last gate on the ridge above the roosting site, well past midnight. They turned their lights off and waited in the car, not wanting to approach the roost until dawn was nearer.

On a clear moonless night, such as this one was, the still night of July 15 (morning of the 16th), 1945, the stars are still brilliant even as, in the time before the sky begins to lighten, the horizon darkens and becomes distinct. They are hunkered down in their seats. The cool air of the night creeps into the car. They are looking out from under the bills of their caps, when a glowing ball appears on the western horizon, like the sun rising in the wrong end of the sky. The light turns from yellow to red, gets very large, and grows alarmingly fast up above the horizon. How big can it get—wavering in color towards purple and then back toward red in a huge column of smoke, or steam, or ash, or whatever? Then the first shock waves wash over them: whump, whump, whump, whump, whump, followed by waves of sound. More shock waves, fumph, fumph, fumph, fumph, fumph; then the column bulging out horizontally at the top, its color subsiding to gray, its shape a mushroom.

Perry and Bill sit there a while without saying a word—no exclamations, no cussing, or long, low whistles, nor do they look at each other.

Finally, Bill turns to Perry and says, "I don't know about you, but if that happens one more time, *I'm* going back to town."

Pete Sinclair

January 1998

O T H E R

ADVENTURE GUIDES

Cross Country Northeast
John R. Fitzgerald Jr.
ISBN: 1-879415-07-0 $12.00

Cross Country Skiing
in Southern California
Eugene Mezereny
ISBN: 1-879415-08-9 $14.00

Great Rock Hits of Hueco Tanks
Paul Piana
ISBN: 1-879415-03-8 $6.95

Mountain Bike Adventures...
MOAB, Utah
Bob Ward
ISBN: 1-879415-11-9 $15.00

The Rogue River Guide
Kevin Keith Tice
ISBN: 1-879415-12-7 $15.00

ADVENTURES, LITERATURE

A Night on the Ground,
A Day in the Open
Doug Robinson
ISBN: 1-879415-14-3 $19.00

Baja Fever:
Journey's into Mexico's Intriguing
Peninsula
Greg Niemann
ISBN:1-879415-19-4 $19.50

High Endeavors
Pat Ament
ISBN: 1-879415-00-3 $12.95

On Mountains and Mountaineers
Mikel Vause
ISBN: 1-879415-06-2 $12.95

Rock and Roses
Mikel Vause, editor
ISBN: 1-879415-01-1 $11.95

ADVENTURES, LITERATURE (CONT.)

The View From the Edge: Life and
Landscapes of Beverly Johnson
Gabriela Zim
ISBN: 1-879415-16-X $17.00

COOKING (BEARLY COOKING)

Cooking with Strawberries
Margaret and Virginia Clark
ISBN: 1-879415-26-7 $10.95

EATING OUT

The Nose Knows: A Sensualist Guide
to great Eating Joints in the Greater
Los Angeles Area
Lloyd McAteer Battista
ISBN: 1-879415-23-2 $13.00

HIKING AND HIKING GUIDES

Backpacking Primer
Lori Saldana
ISBN: 1-879415-13-5 $12.00

Best Hikes of the Marble Mountain
and Russian Wilderness Areas,
California
Art Bernstein
ISBN: 1-879415-18-6 $16.00

Best Hikes of the Trinity Alps (CA)
Art Bernstein
ISBN: 1-879415-05-4 $17.00

Portland Hikes, 2"~ Edition Art
Bernstein and Andrew Jackman
ISBN: 1-879415-22-4 $18.00

So... How Does the Rope Get Up
There, Anyway?
Kathy Myers and Mark Blanchard
ISBN: 1-879415-17-8 $10.00